Emotional Intelligence

Improve Your EQ for Business and Relationships

Unleash The Empath In You!

Millenia Publishing

Dan Coleman

Table Of Contents

This page has been intentionally left blank

(good stuff awaiting you around the corner)

Introduction

Is emotional intelligence as crucial as intellectual intelligence for success and improving your quality of life? Can your emotional intelligence quotient enhance your quality of relationships and give you a contented life? Well, the answer is yes – in fact, it may be more significant than intellectual intelligence! The concept of emotional intelligence has evolved over the years, and it is important to know how it has evolved from being known as social intelligence in the 1930s to emotional strength in the middle of 20th century to today's jargon - emotional intelligence.

So, what is emotional intelligence and why is it so important? Why do you think experts have begun to ask people to work on their emotional intelligence for both personal and professional growth? Studies and surveys show that people who have a high level of emotional intelligence find it easier to manage both their personal and professional lives equally well. They can succeed at work, build stronger and healthier relationships, and accomplish personal and professional goals with ease.

When you can identify, understand, manage and use your emotions in positive ways to rise above challenges, communicate efficiently, alleviate stress, neutralize conflicts and empathize with others, your emotional intelligence is perfect! Do you think emotional intelligence is essential only for people who work in fields that require active communication with the others? Yes? That's not true! Emotional intelligence isn't restricted to a specific work area or people – it is required for everyone. It is the perfect gateway for a well-balanced life in every aspect!

The way you interact with people, the way you behave with your colleagues, the way you respond to strangers or the way you handle stress – emotional intelligence impacts every aspect of your regular day-to-day life. If your emotional intelligence is high, you are fortunate enough to:

- Identify your emotional state

- Analyze and understand the emotional states of people around you

- Engage yourself with people in a way that they are drawn to you

When you can understand the emotions of people, you can use it to empathize, help, achieve and succeed. How do you do it? You will be in a better position to relate to people and situations, work toward healthy relationships both in the personal and professional area, attract success towards self and lead a contented life.

It is a well-known fact that the smartest or brightest people are not always successful in their personal lives – even academically brilliant people might not be successful in their personal lives or professional setups. IQ doesn't always guarantee success in life! Yes, it can help you get a job or into college, but to survive and battle your stress and emotions in those situations, you will need EQ.

Today, you often hear the term Emotional Intelligence in business meetings, within your human resource departments, and in executive boardrooms. Companies prefer people who are people-smart rather than book-smart. A particular survey conducted by a job site found that almost one-third of employers have started to emphasize hiring and promoting people with emotional intelligence, especially after the recession era.

Another survey conducted found that close to 61 percent of employers offer promotions to their employees with higher EQs instead of those with higher IQs, and 59 percent of hiring managers said they wouldn't hire someone with low EQ, even if they had high IQ. They want their employees to be effective decision-makers even when they are under tremendous stress or pressure. They want to hire leaders who can emphasize the needs of clients and colleagues, even when his back is on fire!

Is there a way to improve your emotional intelligence? Yes, the best and the easiest way is by learning to control your thoughts! I know it is easier said than done but with continuous practice, it can be the game changer you were looking for! Most of the emotions we experience occur in an instant and controlling how we feel for that brief moment is difficult. But controlling on how we react to that particular emotion or feeling is possible, as it is focused on our thoughts.

For instance, you may be unable to respond to any situation in an impulse, which most often lands you in trouble, as you tend to say or do something that you regret later. How can you control this emotional reaction? Pause for a few seconds, stop and think! Yes, you have to develop the ability to stop for a few seconds, allowing your emotions to stay under your control, ultimately preventing you from repeating your earlier mistakes.

But what do you do if you cannot hold your opinions back? For instance, you may want to react or respond to a particular situation or scenario, but something or the other refrains you from doing so. In such cases, you question your mind – *will I regret it if I don't say this now?* The answer to the question will tell you whether to react or not.

We're just talking about one method here, and there are many more to help you in this process, but the crucial objective is the same every single time, irrespective of the scenario or people; have power over your thoughts, manage your feelings and make the emotions work in your favor!

This book will provide you with a summary of emotional intelligence and its importance in every facet of your life. The book aims to provide actionable tips and strategies to improve business performance through the practical application of EI. You can also improve your relationships through the types of practical EI mentioned in the book. The book will benefit everyone finding it difficult to control their emotions – both in their personal and professional lives.

If you are someone who wants to do better in your workplace and navigate through complex workplace politics in a better way, you must work on your emotional intelligence. Similarly, if you want to improve your relationship with your spouse, partner or family, you might have to work on your emotional quotient. This book will serve as an effective guide for anyone who would want to understand what emotional intelligence is and the ways it can be useful to comprehend the self in a much better way.

I hope this book serves as an informative and interesting read to you!

Thanks again for purchasing this book. I hope you enjoy it!

Chapter One:

Emotional Intelligence. What is it?

Emma and Daniel had a serious argument with their boss, and they were fuming. When they had both reached their respective houses, one more instance was waiting to provoke their already-hurt emotions further. Daniel's kids had created a mess in his room, which made him yell at them. Meanwhile, Emma's kids had turned their bedroom into a pool of toys and were playing noisily, refusing to go to bed. Instead of yelling at them, Emma chose to sit down with them and politely reasoned with them about their mistakes. She asked them to put the toys back and get to bed. Emma knew that yelling or showing her anger at the kids was of no use, as she wasn't angry with them but at her boss.

Have you noticed the difference in both these individuals while handling their emotions? Emma was able to recognize her emotion and express it differently than Daniel did. To comprehend why these incidents happen, you will need to understand what emotional intelligence is and the role it plays in your regular life.

The first thing to understand is that human beings are intelligent creatures with a quotient of intellectual intelligence or cognitive intelligence, which is most often referred to as IQ. But, there is indeed another level of intelligence quotient in humans, which is more important than the IQ. It is referred to as emotional intelligence, or the emotional quotient. The idea that you and I have these two different quotients has been emerging for close to 30 years now. The terms became popular in the 1990s and have now become common jargon in almost all languages of the world. Many people consider it a naturally alluring construct, but what exactly do they mean when they say "He has been a successful leader for years due to his high emotional intelligence"? The chapter will discuss emotional intelligence in detail.

What is Emotional Intelligence?

In simple words, emotional intelligence defines the level of ability to:

- Identify and understand your emotions and its consecutive reactions, i.e., self-awareness

- Manage, control and adapt to your mood, emotions, responses and reactions, i.e., self-management

- Bind together your emotions to motivate the self to take the right action, follow through, commit and work towards achieving your goals, i.e., motivation

- Recognize other's feelings and emotions, understand them and utilize that knowledge to relate to others in a better manner, i.e., empathy

- Build relationships, relate to social situations, lead the way, settle conflicts and work as a team, i.e., social skills

The ability that allows you to identify and comprehend the emotional feelings of others can be termed emotional intelligence. The understanding you get in this process is completely nonverbal – neither you nor the opposite person says anything out loud, but you determine the feelings only through nonverbal emotions. When you are successful in this attempt, it helps to influence both your thought process (inner world) and the interpersonal relationships (outer world).

Daniel Goleman popularized the term emotional intelligence in 1995, but the first person to refer to said term was Michael Beldoch in 1964. Simply put, emotional intelligence is the ability to recognize, manage and evaluate emotions. It is the capability to observe your own emotions as well as other people's emotions, distinguish between the emotions, label the emotions and use that information to channel an effective thought process and behavioral pattern. But the scientific community doesn't agree with this definition. According to them, emotional intelligence involves recognizing, comprehending and managing emotions!

Researchers wanted to study the neurological area of the human brain that contributes to emotional intelligence. They created the first detailed map of the regions of the brain that contribute to emotional intelligence by studying 152 veterans of Vietnam who were fighting brain injuries. They found that emotional intelligence and general intelligence overlapped significantly, not only in the areas of the brain but also in the behavioral patterns. Veterans who had scored high on general intelligence tests also demonstrated higher performance on measures of emotional intelligence. Many of the same brain regions were found to be crucial for both!

Individuals with high emotional intelligence tend to solve a variety of problems related to emotions quickly and perfectly. These people can perceive the emotions in other's faces and use it as a tool to find a solution to the problem. These individuals can utilize these emotional episodes in their lives to motivate a specific thought process. For instance, the analytical thought process is high when you are sad; anger in certain people can be dangerous, and cheerfulness would result in wanting to mingle with others.

Emotional intelligence is the ability to distinguish emotions, to access and create emotions to assist the thought-process; to comprehend emotions and emotional knowledge; and to pensively control emotions to help emotional and intellectual growth.

Precisely put, there are four parts to emotional intelligence:

- Sensing emotions

- Use emotions to aid thought

- Comprehend emotions

- Regulate emotions

Emotional Intelligence and History

Although the concept of emotional intelligence has been gaining importance and popularity in the past few years, it actually has a much longer history - thousands of years, to be specific.

"All learning has an emotional base." - Plato had written this 2000 years ago and since then many educators, philosophers and scientists have worked to prove or contradict the importance of emotions. But for the most of those two millennia, the generic assumption was that emotions were in the way – a disturbance that keeps humans from making the right decision. They don't help with focus. However, extensive research conducted over the last 30 years proved exactly the opposite.

In the early 1950's, when Abraham Maslow wrote about how people could improve their physical, mental, emotional and spiritual strengths, the human civilization had witnessed the best celebration of humanism since the Renaissance - the Human Potential movement. This became the reason for several major developments in the field of science. New sciences of human capacity were founded in the 1970s and 80s. Peter Salovey was one of these researchers who contributed to the development – he is currently a provost and professor at Yale University. According to him, the last few decades saw a series of changes when it came to beliefs about intelligence and emotions. Initially, intelligence was linked to perfection in an individual, but more studies and researches added that there were more things in life. A long time ago, emotions were considered an eternal punishment, but slowly people realized that they had a substantive value (an independent existence).

Dorothy Van Ghent had mentioned in her book English Novel in 1953 (way before people got the idea that intelligence and emotions could connect) that many Jane Austen characters possessed high emotional intelligence. Around 1966, German psychoanalyst Barbara Lerner believed that women with low emotional intelligence had suffered early separation from their mother, which caused more emotional issues in them when compared to their other counterparts. She suggested that LSD might help women overcome this problem. Wayne Payne was probably the first person to use the term emotional intelligence in his thesis in 1986, where he used the term extensively to argue how important emotional awareness was for the development of children.

John D. Mayer and Peter Salovey, the two psychologists, had introduced the theory of emotional intelligence in 1990 where the concept was formulated, and the way to measure EI was demonstrated in two of the journal articles. They coined the term Emotional Intelligence and described it as,

"A form of social intelligence that involves the ability to monitor one's own and others' feelings and emotions, to discriminate among them, and to use this information to guide one's thinking and action."

It was during this period that IQ (Intellectual Intelligence) was held to high standards and was considered the golden norm for excellence in life. Both the psychologists initiated research programs to explore the significance of the emotional quotient in humans. In a particular study, a group of people was tested on emotional clarity – the ability to recognize and label the mood they were experiencing. These people were then asked to watch an upsetting film, and those who had scored high on the emotional clarity test were able to recover more quickly from the film when compared to the ones who had scored low.

9

Similarly, in another study, it was found that individuals who scored higher in the ability to recognize, understand and assess other's emotions accurately were flexible in adapting to the changes in their respective social environments. They were confidently able to build up supportive social networks in their circle.

Daniel Goleman, a science writer for the New York Times who specialized in behavior and brain research, heard about Mayer and Salovey's work in the 1990s. He had trained at Harvard as a psychologist where he worked with David McClelland who was one among the group of researchers who was more concerned about cognitive intelligence. McClellan believed that cognitive intelligence is a must-have for an individual to be successful in life, but Goleman didn't agree with his concept. According to him, cognitive intelligence doesn't guarantee business success, but emotional intelligence does. This eventually led to his book *Emotional Intelligence: Why it Can Matter More Than IQ.*

Goleman explained that emotionally intelligent individuals came with four major characteristics:

- The ability to understand their own emotions (self-awareness)

- The ability to manage their emotions (self-management)

- The ability to empathize with other people's emotions (social awareness)

- The ability to handle other people's emotions (social skills)

He had to fight hard to prove these because it was the days when people believed that IQ is more important than emotions. There was a hot debate where few argued that IQ is genetic, while few others believed that it was possible to acquire a higher IQ with experience. But it all changed in 1995 when Goleman introduced new reports of research that mentioned emotional intelligence as an important ingredient to succeed in life. His work included many other scientific developments (in the field of neuroscience, which explored about how emotions are usually regulated in the brain since infancy!)

Three Models of Emotional Intelligence

After a series of research done on emotional intelligence by John Mayer, Peter Salovey, Daniel Goleman and Konstantin Vasily Petrides, the three models of emotional intelligence were introduced. They are:

- The Ability Model

- The Mixed Model

- The Trait Model

But even today, most people focus on the Mixed Model derived and explained by Daniel Goleman.

Ability Model

John Mayer, University of New Hampshire and Peter Salovey, Yale University had together developed this model of emotional intelligence. They defined emotional intelligence as the ability to reason out one's emotions and use them to enhance the thinking process. To determine a person's emotional quotient, he has to be evaluated in four separate but interlinked abilities. They are:

- Perceiving emotions (comprehend nonverbal signs or cues – facial expressions or body language)

- Reason with emotions (use the emotions to encourage the right mode of thinking and cognitive action)

11

- Understand emotions (ability to interpret the emotions of people around you. For instance, if a person is angry you should be able to understand if his anger is towards you or the situation)

- Manage emotions (regulate the emotions and respond consistently and appropriately)

In this model, it is established that a person will remain open to emotional signals as long as those signals do not hurt him; however, if the emotions were to cause pain, he will block those emotions that overwhelm him. This response is measured through the MSCEIT (Mayer-Salovey-Caruso Emotional Intelligence Test), which is based on problem-solving items based on emotions.

Mixed Model

David Goleman developed this model based on emotional intelligence and other personality traits that are neither related to intelligence or emotions. He used five categories or components to describe emotional intelligence:

- Self-Awareness (self-confidence and emotional awareness – the ability to recognize feelings)

- Self-Regulation (controlling impulsive behaviors, innovation – creative thinking, trustworthiness – honesty & integrity, conscientiousness – taking responsibility for one's actions and, adaptability – ability to handle changes)

- Motivation (Drive – sticking to goals even in times of pressure or obstacles, commitment – holding on to integrity, initiative – taking the lead, optimism – looking to improve consistently)

- Empathy (understanding other's emotions, diversity –

12

building relationships with people different from you, service orientation – ability to anticipate other's needs, political awareness)

- Social Skills (Communication skills, leadership, handling conflicts)

The Emotional Competency Inventory developed by Goleman helps measure the emotional intelligence in this model. You can also take the emotional intelligence appraisal for a self assessment.

Trait Model

Konstantin Vasily Petrides published this model recently in 2009 where he defines emotional intelligence as the self-perception of an individual's emotional abilities that include both the self-perceived and behavioral abilities. He defined his model as "a constellation of emotional self-perceptions located at the lower levels of personality."

The two components that determine a person's emotional intelligence are:

- The perception and understanding of one's emotions

- The use of personality framework to study the trait emotional intelligence.

The respondent's self-report is the way to measure this model, and it can be done through the TEIQue (Trait Emotional Questionnaire).

Comparison of the other Emotional Intelligence Models

While you look at the intricacies of all the models, all of them touch on comprehending your emotions, taking control of your feelings, and applying the result to improve your ability to interact with others.

	Self-Awareness	Self-Management	Application
Ability Model	Perceive Understand	Utilize	Manage Regulate
Mixed Model	Self-awareness	Self-management	Being aware of other's emotions Relationships
Trait Model	Understanding Perception	Study	Personality Framework

A high IQ can get you onto a shortlist of candidates for a particular job but for you to make an impact in the interview process; you will need the required emotional intelligence. Emotional intelligence is essential in one's day-to-day life but if you are going to ask – which is better to have – IQ or EQ? Then it is a wrong question, as the two bits of intelligence should complement each other for an individual to lead a higher quality of life!

Chapter Two: Why Emotional Intelligence Is Important To You

The knowledge of emotions should have been taught to us when we were young, but unfortunately, we are taught very little about things that matter. Instead of emphasizing to work on general intelligence (or cognitive ability), we should have been given more knowledge on how to be emotionally sound. Recent studies and researches conducted by psychologists show that one's overall intelligence quotient is directly associated with their emotional intelligence.

When your consciousness is emotionally sound, you will be in a better position to perform and generate the expected results when they matter the most. The undeniable fact here is – you are judged based on your emotions. Your lips can lie but your eyes cannot! For instance, if you are guilty of a crime that you never committed, your emotions will speak an entirely different language. For example, if you are ashamed when one of your fellow species had heinously molested and murdered a helpless girl, your emotions bubble up differently. Though you were not the one who committed the crime, you take the guilt upon yourself because it was one of your kind who did it!

"He liked to observe emotions; they were like red lanterns strung along the dark unknown of another's personality. Marking vulnerable points." – Ayn Rand

When you meet a person, the first thing you tend to (or rather your mind tends to) notice is non-verbal cues – the facial expression, the body language and the emotional display of the other person. This happens even before the opposite person opens his mouth to speak.

Why Is It So Important? How Can It Impact Your Life?

Emotions play a critical role in every single person's life, and so does the impact it has on every aspect of the person's life. Emotional intelligence can impact some or all of the following areas in your life:

Work Life and Performance

Emotional intelligence can help you steer social complications in the workplace. It can help you guide and inspire others, and at the same time help you to excel in your career. Today, the majority of organizations are assessing their candidates based on emotional intelligence. EQ test is equally important as the technical assessment a candidate is required to take for his or her candidature to get through the selection process.

Physical Health

Most people get into serious health issues, as they are unable to handle their stress levels. If you are not in a position to manage and take control of your stress, you invite many health issues like:

- Blood pressure

- Weak immune system

- Infertility issues

- Increase in the risk of stroke and heart attack

If you want to improve your emotional intelligence, you must first learn to handle stress and identify ways to relieve any excess stress.

Your ability to take care of your health and manage your stress has an unbelievable impact on your overall wellness. When you lead a stress-free life, you will have a higher emotional IQ. How do you manage this? You can do it only when you are aware of your emotional state, identify the emotions you are going through and take steps to act accordingly to reduce the negative reaction to your own emotions.

Mental Health

Uncontrolled stress not only impacts your physical health but also affects your mental health, which makes you vulnerable to depression and anxiety. When you are not able to comprehend and regulate your emotions, you tend to experience mood swings more often. Similarly, the inability to establish strong relationships can leave you feeling cut off and forlorn.

Emotional intelligence can help change the way we look at life – it can help with a positive attitude that can reduce the anxiety and avoid mood swings (which in most cases leads to depression). A high level of emotional intelligence is directly related to positive thoughts and happy life.

Relationships

When you can understand your emotions and control them, you are in a better position to express your feelings and understand how others feel. This makes your communication effective and builds stronger relationships, not just in your personal life but also in your professional environment.

Constructive communication is all that matters, and you can do it when you take control of your emotions and regulate them in the correct way. Your relationships become fulfilling when you can comprehend their feelings, understand their needs and work on the responses accordingly.

Conflict Management

You can resolve conflicts much easily or avoid them even before they start when you can differentiate between people's emotions and empathize with their perception of things. You also become better at negotiation when your ability to understand the wants and desires of others is good. If you can perceive what a person wants, it is much easier to give!

Ability to Succeed

When your emotional intelligence is high, your self-motivation is equally high as it increases your confidence, reduces your act of postponing things and improves your ability to concentrate on a particular goal. Confidence and a positive attitude towards everything in life allow you to create much better support networks, conquer setbacks and continue with a better, resilient stance. When you can look for long-term results, your ability to succeed naturally increases.

Positive Leadership

Individuals with higher emotional intelligence make better leaders, as their ability to comprehend the motivational factor of others, positively connect with the team and weave a strong bond with everyone in the workplace is extraordinary. A leader can succeed only when he is aware of his people's needs and can gratify the needs. This ultimately gives his people the expected work satisfaction leading to higher performance.

Building stronger teams by tactically utilizing the emotional diversity of the team members to benefit the team as a whole is only possible with an intelligent and emotionally strong leader.

Emotional Quotient in Children

Many studies have indicated a strong connection between the children's behavior in the classroom and their emotional intelligence. Kids with low emotional intelligence are found to struggle with concentration. They also have problems communicating their emotions. These often lead to aggressive behavior toward their classmates resulting in bullying. These behavioral patterns are said to start during preschool and elementary school, which tend to increase with time.

Emotional intelligence is not in one's genes or something that comes naturally, as most of the components related to EQ are learned in social environments (schools, churches, etc.). School is where kids learn to communicate emotions, express their feelings, empathize and resolve conflicts with their friends. As earlier research already proved that emotional intelligence has a direct impact on intellectual intelligence, a better EQ can help in better academic scores. It is therefore essential to include emotional intelligence in school programs not just to improve the classroom environment but also to help the children identify and regulate their own emotions.

Though emotional intelligence is not completely understood, it cannot be denied that emotions play a crucial role in impacting the overall quality of one's professional and personal life. And this becomes even more critical when compared to the intelligence factor of the brain. There are a lot of technologies and tools that can help you train and master the information. But, ultimately the ability to learn, manage and master your emotions and the emotions of those around you is completely dependent on yourself.

Controlling Your Emotions

As mentioned earlier, emotional intelligence is not inborn – it can be learned. No matter how old you are, it is never too late to work on your emotional quotient to ensure you have a happier and better life.

Get in Touch With Your Feelings

Never lose touch with your emotions; observe your feelings! Most often we are too busy worrying about what is to be done or what can be done to make things better. Ignoring your emotions doesn't help, but instead, it is necessary to take good care of your emotions. Suppressing your emotions can be dangerous and at times can make things worse. When you suppress your emotions, you are bottling them up, and one fine day they may become so uncontrollable that they erupt, like hot molten lava from a volcano.

Why do you have an emotional reaction to something? This could be because you have some issues in that area lying there, unresolved. So, next time you experience a negative emotion, instead of trying to put the emotions behind you, relax and think about why you are going through that particular emotion. Take a deep breath and jot down all the emotions you are experiencing and their likely reasons for existence. When you read what you have written, you can discover the emotions that trigger you the most and the reasons behind it. You can then think about the different ways to deal with the root cause.

Respond; Don't React

What is the difference between responding and reacting? When you respond, you consciously pay attention to your feelings and decide

20

how to behave based on the scenario. So, it is a conscious process. But when you react, you are relieving or expressing an emotion for a brief moment. It is an unconscious process. For instance, when you are provoked, you instantly react, but when you consciously respond, the effect is much better!

How can you do this? When you are aware of your emotional triggers, you can always think about how to behave when such a situation arises again. For instance, you may always react bluntly to your colleagues at the office whenever you are stressed. Think about the triggers that made you react that way to your colleague and behave a bit differently the next time such a situation occurs. Maybe you can tell your colleague to leave you alone for a moment to calm down, or you can tell them that you will come back to them later, once you're feeling better.

Be Humble and Wise

Believing in yourself is good, but don't make the mistake of going overboard by being overconfident til the point you're unable to see your faults. It is during such instances that you become caught in emotional tangles when you see that the other person is unable to meet your expectation.

Look at it from a different angle – imagine yourself in the other person's shoes and try to think or feel the way they would. Then ask yourself – Would I be doing this? Would I react this way in such a scenario? This will naturally stop you from judging others and instead encourage you to try to understand their thoughts and emotions more. This can help you deal with the issue in a much more reasonable manner.

Be humble enough to accept that you aren't better than anyone and wise enough to recognize that you are different from the others.

Benefits and Uses

Your success doesn't only depend on your ability to acquire a particular skill, but it also depends on how you connect with others. To make connections and show the positive aspects of your personality, you need to be aware of the vulnerable points – emotions! Being aware is not enough; you should be able to demonstrate the ability to pick up these emotional points in one's behavior. When you can identify the emotions, you can deal with the person in a much better way. You can comprehend the person's behavioral patterns, their limitations and their vulnerabilities. How can all this happen? When you take active steps to work on your emotional quotient, you can make this happen. As Daniel Goleman mentioned, you must first analyze, manage, motivate and empathize.

Emotional Intelligence has been a vast area of research for many scientists and experts. Some say that creativity and innovation are directly associated with your emotions. Don't forget – emotional intelligence is not jargon used in psychology; it is a fundamental and essential part of your life! When you are emotionally intelligent, you don't allow stress to overpower you and therefore are already on a path of leading a better life, without even you noticing it.

As Aristotle quoted in his classic *The Art of Rhetoric*, 2000 years ago, "ANYBODY can become angry, that is easy; but to be angry with the right person, and to the right degree, and at the right time, and for the right purpose, and in the right way, that is not within everybody's power, and that is not easy." Getting angry is easy, but doing it the right way, by taking control of your emotions, is not easy. You need to practice!

Why IQ Isn't the Only Determinant of Success

When there's an important debate that contrasts on the relative importance of emotional intelligence and cognitive intelligence, the one question that gets into the heart of the debate is – what is more important in determining the success of life – street smarts or book smarts? People who support book smarts will suggest that IQ plays a major role in determining life's success, whereas those who support street smarts would suggest the EI/EQ (emotional intelligence) is much more important than IQ. So, which is important?

Daniel Goleman suggested that emotional intelligence may be more important than IQ and he enclosed scientific evidence for the same. Yes, few psychologists believe that the conventional way of measuring IQ is slender and therefore doesn't cover the entire range of human intelligence. For instance, psychologist Howard Gardner suggested that intelligence is not a single ability, but there are multiple facets of intelligence. People might have strengths in many of these facets of intelligence. This proves that general intelligence or cognitive quotient is not the only one to be looked at.

Few experts believed that the capability to comprehend and articulate emotions could play an equal role with general intelligence. How is IQ measured and tested? Intellectual intelligence or cognitive intelligence is a number that is derived from a standardized intelligence test (IQ tests). How are the scores calculated? In the original IQ tests, the individual's mental age was divided by his or her chronological age and multiplied by 100. For example, a kid whose chronological age is 10 and mental age is 15 will have an IQ of 150. But today, most IQ tests calculate the scores by comparing the score of the person who had taken the test with the scores of other people in the same age group. What are the abilities represented by IQ?

- World knowledge

- Spatial and visual processing

- Quantitative memory

- Fluid reasoning

- Short-term memory and working memory

Measuring the person's level of emotional intelligence by identifying his ability to perceive, control, evaluate and express emotions is referred to as the emotional quotient. This concept is now the latest buzzword not only in workplaces but also at education centers as more experts feel the necessity for children to learn the emotional quotient from their young age. What are the abilities represented by EQ?

- Recognizing emotions

- Evaluating other's feelings

- Taking control of one's own emotions

- Perceiving other's feelings

- Facilitating social interactions using these emotions

- Empathizing and relating to other's feelings

The journey of the concept of emotional intelligence started from taking its place in academic journals to being recognized as a well-known term that affects the walks of everyone's life. It is now possible to help boost your kid's emotional intelligence by enrolling them in SEL (social and emotional learning) programs, buying them toys that can help enhance their emotion quotient, etc. Few schools in the United States have already added SEL as a part of their curriculum requirement.

There was a time when IQ was viewed as the major determinant of success, and people with high IQs were believed to be successful in leading an accomplished life. But when a few critics stepped in with theories that mentioned emotions and emotional thinking, a full-on debate started. Scientific evidence, neurological research and a series of studies showed that emotional intelligence is equally or perhaps more important than IQ.

You cannot deny that IQ is still an important element for success, especially in academics. To add on to this, EQ also influences many things for positive development and attitude toward life. Today's business world looks at emotional intelligence as a strong construct to taste success. EQ tests have become mandatory in most companies and multiple pieces of research show that people with high EQ make strong and potential leaders.

For instance, one particular insurance organization found that emotional intelligence could play a critical role in being successful in the sales domain. Employees who had high measures of emotional intelligence sold policies worth $114,000 (on average) while sales employees who had a lower measure off emotional intelligence abilities such as self-confidence, empathy and initiative could sell only $54,000 (on average) premiums.

Succeeding in life doesn't involve one or two factors – there are many to it, and without a doubt, both EQ and IQ play critical roles in influencing the overall success of your work life. It also handles much more important things such as wellness, happiness and health. Instead of focusing on factors with major influence, it is always wise to learn and improve your skills in multiple areas. Therefore, along with focusing on your cognitive abilities, it is also equally important to get ahold of emotional and social skills that might serve you well in various areas of your life.

Chapter Three: The Driving Force

The foundation for future learning is established from the time a child is born until he or she turns six. It is during this time that the changeover from dependence to independence happens for the child. The child begins to develop an emotional blueprint that notifies him or her on every aspect of his or her life. When the child is guided to identify and manage his emotions at this age, the emotional quotient tends to get stronger over time. The ability to understand and manage one's feelings is the driving force for social and intellectual accomplishment and can, therefore, be considered as the strongest pointer for success.

Irrespective of the temperamental or genetic tendency with which a child is born, it is possible to effectively cultivate emotional intelligence in the child before he gets into elementary school. Concentrating on this area at a much earlier stage (infancy) can make a difference in the kid's outlook toward life. When children receive the gift of mindfulness in the early stages of life, they develop important assets such as:

- Kindness

- Creativity

- Concentration

- Competency

- Self-advocacy

- Self-control

- Inquisitiveness

- Proficiency

- Problem-solving

- Managing fears and worries

When the child is trained on emotional intelligence, he or she can maximize his or her potential and build resilience.

Understanding Temperament

The CEO of Six Seconds, Joshua Freeman, maintains an interesting blog: "Emotions, feelings and moods – Does anybody know the difference?" The difference between the three is only a matter of time.

Emotions are chemicals that are released in response to your interpretation of a particular trigger. They last for only 6 seconds.

Feelings are the outcome of your emotions, i.e., when you let your emotions sink in; you begin to feel the outcome of the emotion. The chemicals of the emotion are processed in your bodies and brain; therefore, feelings are saturated in the cognitive process. Feelings last longer than emotions.

Moods are a collection of inputs that aren't tied to a specific incident but are rather generalized. So many different factors influence your mood – physiology (how healthy you are, what you eat, how you exercise, how you sleep, etc.), environment (climate, people, noise, etc.) and mental state (current emotions, current focus, etc.). Unlike emotions and feelings, moods can last for a much longer period – minutes, hours or even days.

According to this model, momentary emotions only gain importance over time, but unfortunately, this won't work well to increase your emotional intelligence. You will need to understand the temperament of the person to determine his emotional responses that are usually habitual. Why is it so? Temperament is a part of one's personality, and it can last longer than days – it can last a lifetime!

Temperaments that are usually set at the time of birth are source points for the reaction to an emotional trigger. When you understand one's temperament, you get to know his emotions that are usually habituated. This will ultimately reveal to you the further course of reaction of the person. But is it possible to change your temperament? For example: Is it possible to change the temperament of an individual who is highly unpredictable or someone who is extremely shy? Does our biology fix the emotional blueprint? Is it possible for an extremely shy kid to grow into a confident adult?

The neuro-biochemistry shreds of evidence of various temperaments prove that temperament is not destiny. Though genetic heritage bestows you with a series of emotional set points that determine your temperament, the circuit system of the brain involved is unusually malleable and can be influenced. The emotional lessons taught in early childhood can have a deep impact in either intensifying or nullifying an inborn predisposition. Early experiences can have a lasting effect in carving the neural pathways of the individual.

For example, a child whose natural temperament is timidity will grow into a delicate adult if the parents have been protecting her since childhood. She will not be able to manage even mild stress, as her neural circuitry makes her more reactive. From the time she was born, her heartbeat would have increased rapidly in response to new or strange scenarios. This particular response lies within her and develops into lifelong timidity. She will look at any new person or scenario as a potential threat!

But if her parents gradually encourage their naturally timid child by providing him or her with the confidence to handle new situations, this may turn into a corrective measure to get rid of their fear which might otherwise exist for life. Parents shouldn't be judgmental or critical but rather offer their emotional support by talking to the child about her feelings and how she needs to understand, analyze and address them. Offering problem-solving help when she is in an emotional mess and guiding her on what needs to be done when she is pulled down by negative or difficult emotions is necessary.

It is often seen that people who had traumatic emotional experiences during their childhood suffer a series of mental health issues – mild or severe. In the most serious of cases, even psychotherapy doesn't work. This is why emotional intelligence is important. Every key skill of EQ has critical periods of development – the time when the child is prepared to develop these emotional abilities. If the appropriate time window is missed, it becomes more difficult to learn them later, but not impossible.

This huge carving and pruning of neural circuits during childhood may be the reason why early emotional suffering and hardship have insidious and continual effects in adulthood, where psychotherapy also takes a much longer time to affect these neural patterns. Even after continuous therapies, these patterns tend to remain as underlying propensities that have the natural tendency to behave in a particular manner though relearned responses. New insights are superimposed over this layer. Therefore, it is crucial to be prepared when young, as the remedy for every solution is linked to how you were prepared for the world when you were young.

The Key Driver Behind Emotions

When you try to separate feeling and thinking, everything becomes artificial. Emotions that ultimately lead to feelings drive every single thing. The author of *Molecules of Emotion,* Candace Pert, (who was also a leading neurobiologist) confirmed that thinking occurs in the body and brain, while all other kinds of information (feelings, ideas and even spiritual impulses) are processed all through the body. The brain is the processing power, but it is not the driving force of the system.

After the groundbreaking research conducted on emotional intelligence by Mayer and Salovey, the concept of EQ is still young. Even after 25 years, we continue to define basic intelligence when there are multiple intelligences to be discussed. The key to getting through more scientific evaluations is by refining the research of development, its effects and the assessment process. Dr. Salovey mentions the same, *"The real challenge is to show that emotional intelligence matters over-and-above psychological constructs that have been measured for decades, like personality and IQ. I believe that emotional intelligence holds this promise."*

Your emotions are driven by your temperament, and most of the emotions you display are habitual due to your behavioral patterns. When you can identify your temperament, you can understand why you show particular emotions in specific scenarios. Most of the time, the patterns are repetitive, and when you can recognize this, you gain better control over your emotions and instead of reacting, you begin to respond. You consciously attempt to behave in a particular way that works well for both you and the people around you. When you begin to gauge your emotional pattern, you can manage the flow of emotions and encourage (and motivate) yourself to work towards betterment.

For instance, when you tend to get angry at the slightest provocation, you need to find the key force that is driving this emotion in you. In other words, the trigger point that is pushing this emotion in you! You may have to calm down, relax and rewind. Is it the person you are angry with? Or is it the thing that he said which provoked you? Or is it both? When you begin to question yourself, the more you tend to observe and work accordingly!

Neuroscience

If you need to work on your emotional intelligence, you will first have to understand the neuroscience behind it. When you understand how the brain works, you can gain a clearer picture of how to comprehend and develop your emotional intelligence quotient.

Earlier, the models in psychology discussed described the behavioral pattern of humans concerning stimulus and response. On the other hand, today's advancements in neuroscience and psychology show that there are a series of stages that fall between the stimulus and response. The information is filtered in the initial stage via your attitude(s) before it gets processed as emotions, thoughts and feelings. The response to this processed information is your behavior. This behavior produces an outcome.

You can summarize the stages as follows:

- Stimulus

- Attitude/pattern match

- Feeling

- Emotion

- Thinking/thought process

- Behavior/habit

- Outcome/performance

It is referred to by the acronym SAFE-T!

Scientific research shows that not one, but many different regions of the brain facilitate the emotional quotient in human beings.

The brain is the management while the heart is the workforce representative. The brain is comprised of three major sections:

- Primate brain (the area responsible for giving you the hunches; deals with rapid processing of information)

- Mammalian brain (your habits, memory, etc. come from this area)

- Reptilian brain (your motions and autonomic functions come from this area)

When you develop a clear insight into the workings of the brain, you can infer how to develop your emotional intelligence and work on it. For instance, though most people know what they should be doing, they don't put this into practice, i.e., they know they have to do a certain thing, but they don't *do it*. The limbic brain (emotional) learns that a particular thing needs to be done, but it can only learn to do it by action (doing). So, if you want to turn your good intentions into behavior, you will have to habituate it by practicing regularly through physical experience and rehearsal.

Chapter Four: Emotional Intelligence at The Workplace

Steve, a successful manager, was a well-known figure in his organization for his ability to handle and resolve tough organizational problems and show results. He was excellent in evaluating situations, decision-making and for taking ownership of the projects he handled.

The man quickly climbed up the ladder, from being a module lead to delivery head, and was starting to take up more senior roles in the company. He was able to taste success in every step. As he was doing well in every role he was given, he persisted to influence the senior leadership team of the organization to increase his functional responsibilities. He wanted to be given bigger and tougher organizational issues to handle and resolve. His perseverance and hard work gave him room to rise higher in the senior ranks of the management.

Steve was pretty open when it came to his goal – he made it clear that his career objective was to get into the executive suite. He had no secrets! He was confident that he would eventually get to that rank and there were many people in the organization that believed that it was certain. However, Steve didn't get to that place – he didn't get the executive suite. He felt saturated as his career came to a halt – the senior leadership team had reassigned most of his work responsibilities to other managers.

What happened? What went wrong? Why did his career stall? Why was there a sudden swerve in his career path?

The gossip that floated around the organization was that his decline centered on his micromanagement abilities. He used to micromanage his team and peers when he was at the lower levels of the management. This behavior continued when he rose up the ladder, and he started to micromanage his managers, which included even the best talents. He had problems giving them their independent authority because the managers were unable to finish the duties assigned to them.

The inability to delegate authority to his managers led to his downfall. Micromanagement might work at lower levels but when the organizational scope grows, this behavior will get problematic. Steve's style of managing didn't work for the larger role he had taken up, and the result was drastic. He accumulated huge budget shortfalls as he struggled to meet his objectives. He couldn't handle the responsibilities given to him efficiently.

The gossip was, in fact, accurate but only to an extent. Steve's inability to delegate authority and his tendency to micromanage were only the symptoms – there was a much bigger problem! The root of Steve's issue stemmed from the fact that he lacked emotional intelligence! Emotional intelligence is a must-have quality if you want to become an efficient and successful leader. When the leader can identify his emotions and manage them, he gradually gets to a stage where he gains the ability to perceive other's emotions, gauge them, empathize and use it to his advantage for the benefit of the team and organization. This is when he earns credibility from his entire team.

Why is emotional intelligence more important than personality in the work environment?

The rise and fall of Steve as a manager proves why it is important for leaders to have emotional intelligence. The inability to understand and regulate his own emotions led to Steve's downfall. Since he couldn't understand his own emotions and manage them, he wasn't able to understand his team either. This lack of self-awareness became the cause of all his problems.

Why was his emotional intelligence crippled? What was the issue? Steve's fear was his emotional deficiency. But what was his fear about?

Steve feared that if he didn't micromanage things, he would start to lose control of his organizational area. He felt that this might lead him to a stage where he may have problems finishing the responsibilities given to him. He also had a fear of being replaced by his managers if they were perfect in their job, so he restrained from giving them the authority that was rightfully theirs. He felt that if he gave them authority, then he would have no control over them.

This attitude of Steve became his enemy as it proved to hinder his path to success. When he refrained from giving authorities to his manager, the entire burden of decision-making and budget allocation fell on his shoulders. The operations slowed down and ultimately came to a grinding halt when taking decisions took time. Experienced and talented managers who had the capability of taking significant decisions realized that Steve's head nod was a must for anything and everything.

This ultimately frustrated the managers and they felt that Steve was interfering too much with their key responsibilities and operations. Steve started losing his best managers when they took other job opportunities. The ones who remained in his team made sure they stayed out of his way, rather than focusing on generating the best results for their respective projects or teams.

When the senior management team noticed this, they felt that Steve did not have the leadership qualities to handle bigger teams. They concluded that he lacked the temperament and ability to handle his managers effectively. The promotion that was meant for Steve went to another manager who knew how to work with a team of a senior crowd. Steve's lack of emotional intelligence spoiled his goal of reaching the executive suite.

To be an efficient and accepted leader, one must possess effective management skills. To gain this, he or she should be aware of his or her own emotions and also be able to perceive, empathize and manage other's emotions accordingly. Emotional intelligence does this and is therefore a crucial skill for leadership roles.

The story of Steve is quite common in many organizations. An individual who does extremely well in middle management level stumbles when he heads to the senior management level. For some, this hiccup starts quite early, especially during their initial stages of leadership development.

Leaders will need emotional intelligence to keep out the negative emotions from the team. This will help them produce better outcomes and results. When there is a lack of emotional control, the team is crippled with poor productivity, more absenteeism, strained relationships at work, unattained business goals and dreadful organizational turnover.

Workplace Intelligence

Even today, most companies focus more on hard skills (education, experience, domain knowledge and technical hands-on) and personality trait assessments when it comes to their selection process. Empathy, stress management, social acumen, assertiveness and political acumen are some of the competencies that are essential for a workplace scenario. Unfortunately, these are not focused on in training & development programs or measured when it comes to the candidate's selection process. But these are the crucial factors for success that shouldn't be ignored as they can have a direct impact on the employee's outcome.

There have been studies and research conducted that have proved the importance of emotional intelligence in a workplace environment. Most of these researches have unboxed the following stories of success:

- A study conducted by Hay Group proved that salespeople with high emotional intelligence had generated twice the revenue when compared to people who had below average or average scores in EQ. The study was done on 44 Fortune 500 companies.

- Another study showed that technical programmers who had displayed the top ten percent of competency in emotional intelligence could develop software three times quicker than programmers who had lower competency.

- Salespeople with high emotional intelligence did 18 percent better than salespeople with lower emotional intelligence in a Fortune 500 company that deals with financial services.

- The Dallas Corporation conducted a study recently, where they measured the productivity of their employees. Employees who scored high in emotional intelligence were 20 times more productive than employees who had lower scores in EQ.

- A Fortune 500 company in Texas had earlier used personality assessments in their candidate selection process, but it provided little results. Later they turned to emotional intelligence training and development program and included the selection assessment process based on emotional intelligence. The results were astonishing, as they were able to increase retention by 67 percent in the first year ($32 million, in addition to reduced turnover costs and increased sale revenues)

- After implementing an EQ screening assessment process, a large city hospital was able to reduce their attrition rate in nursing (critical care unit) from 65 percent to 15 percent within 18 months of its implementation.

- A community bank that cut off 30 percent of its staff due to slow economy assessed the emotional intelligence of the remaining employees and placed them in roles that suited their competencies. Today, the bank is turning in a better performance with fewer staff.

Emotional Intelligence Competencies for Success in the Workplace

The combined effects of cognitive ability, standard personality traits and technical skills are important to succeed in a professional career. Yet two major emotional intelligence competencies prove to contribute more to workplace success. These include:

- Social competencies

- Personal competencies

Social Competencies

This particular set of skills helps determine how you handle relationships (inter-personal relationships) in the work environment. The skills desired are:

- Instinct and empathy

- Political insight and social skills

Instinct and empathy deal with your alertness and awareness of the emotions, feelings, concerns and needs of others. This competency is crucial when it comes to workplaces for the following reasons:

- You will need to understand others by using your intuitive ability to perceive the feelings and perspectives of the other person. When you show active interests in their concerns and needs, you naturally begin to empathize.

- This will help you achieve customer satisfaction as you are in line with the customer's needs. You can foresee, identify and meet their needs, thereby leading to excellent customer service orientation.

- When you can sense what others require to grow, master and develop their strengths, your development skills will begin to improve.

- The ability to handle people lets you cultivate opportunities within the diversity, thereby maximizing the team efforts.

Political insights and social skills give you the gift of persuading responses and results that you desire from the others. When you are skilled in this area, you can:

- Influence your team for better results by using effective persuasion techniques

- Communicate effectively by sending clear and influential messages that can be easily understood.

- Inspire and guide more people or a group of people, thereby improving your leadership quality.

- Serve as a change catalyst in the workplace and ensure you initiate and manage change for the betterment of the team and organization.

- Resolve conflicts in the team by negotiating and solving disagreements with people. Sometimes, you have to agree to disagree to avoid conflict for the sake of the team or the project.

- Nurture influential relationships by building bonds for the success of the business/

- Cooperate and collaborate by working together toward shared goals with business partners and colleagues.

- Working as a team to pursue collective goals by creating successful interactions between two or more teams.

Personal Competencies

This particular set of skills helps you manage yourself by creating awareness within you. They are:

- Self-awareness

- Self-regulation

- Self-acceptation

Self-awareness allows you to know your internal state of mind, gut instincts, inclinations and resources. When you can identify yourself, you can:

- Identify your emotions and the effects it can cause on you and the people around you. When you know the impact it can cause, you tend to be more cautious and work on your emotional awareness.

- Assess yourself accurately as you know your limitations and strengths.

- Know your capabilities and be confident in your self-worth, thereby increasing your confidence level.

Self-Regulation helps you to manage your impulses, resource abilities and the internal state of mind. This can prove worthy at your workplace, as you can:

- Manage your disturbing emotions and impulses, giving you more power over your self-control.

- Maintain excellent standards of integrity and honesty, enabling people to trust you and your work.

- Be accountable for your performance and take responsibility for your actions as your conscientiousness is perfectly in line.

- Stay comfortable and open to new ideas, information and approaches which most likely lead to innovation in the workplace.

Motivation and self-expectations are the driving forces that guide you to reach your goals. It facilitates and gives you the drive:

- To achieve as you strive harder to meet the standard of excellence that is imposed upon you.

- To align yourself with the goals of the organization and commit towards the team's success.

- To take the initiative and additional responsibilities within the scope of opportunities without being told.

- To be optimistic about pursuing your goals, despite the hindrance and difficulties you come across.

Managing Workplace Conflict With Emotional Intelligence

I have a person on my team, and I cannot stand the sight of her. I know it's absurd, especially when she's my colleague, but she is self-centered, jealous, full of negativity and worst of all, she constantly badmouths anyone and everyone. She cannot keep her mouth shut. There have been times when I don't respond to her when she talks about her work or talks badly about the other team members. I wanted to see how long she would continue her rambling, but to my surprise, she moves from topic to topic – an amazing talent! Seriously, her complete lack of emotional intelligence stresses me out totally.

I can feel my blood pressure rising whenever she walks toward my cubicle. It emotionally exhausts me, and I feel my energy draining away completely. If I don't act quickly on this, sooner or later I would end up in an open conflict with her. I wanted to do something, but I didn't know what to do. How do I handle this situation at my workplace? I wanted to avoid a possible conflict and at the same time save myself from her incessant talking.

I decided to talk to her about her non-stop yapping as I felt she was completely unaware of how it was making me feel. So, unless I am honest with her, I cannot be angry with her, as she didn't know it was disturbing me. Surprisingly, the discussion went well. Though it was not a friendly chat, it did go well as she understood where I was coming from when I was honest with her. After the conversation, she made an effort to set things right, and she was doing a lot better. I was relieved of her backbiting and rambling sessions.

But still, I could feel the frustration mounting up whenever she spoke to me, as the negative vibes weren't completely gone. Though she had considerably reduced her ranting sessions with me, her habit didn't stop her from doing so completely. I kept telling myself to forgive her, move on and start afresh, but I couldn't forgive her and continue. I didn't know what to do next.

This is one among many instances that are quite common in the workplace. Handling such situations requires emotional strength and intelligence.

A study conducted by the University of Munich mentioned emotional and decisional forgiveness. It was a forgiveness experiment involving 42 undergraduate students. Scenarios describing a person's behavior were presented to them, and they were given a list of words that included negative words (such as lazy, selfish, jealous, etc.). They were then divided into three groups, and separate instructions were given to them.

The first group was asked to think about their feelings and thoughts about the person and the scenario. The second group was asked to think about the person as an individual and not the desire for any payback. The third group was instructed to practice empathy actively and wish for the person in the scenario to have healing, positive experiences. Based on the emotions or thoughts they felt for the person and the scenario, they were finally asked to pick some words from the list given. The third group, who were asked to practice empathy, was able to move on as they remembered very few words linked to the person's behavior.

This was when I understood the difference between emotional forgiveness and decisional forgiveness. When you make a rational decision to forgive someone, you force your system to do it. Like how I had forced myself to forgive my colleague. But when it comes to emotional forgiveness, you go one step further by replacing your unmoved negative thoughts with positive thoughts while at the same time forgiving them. For instance, you wish good things to happen to them, instead of thinking, *"I forgive you, leave my sight."* This was what was missing in my case – I forced myself to forgive her, although the negative thoughts about her were still lingering in my head.

I decided to follow the German University's experiment – I started to think about my feelings and thoughts about my colleague. I then told myself that I had to forgive her and move on, but I got stuck. I wasn't doing enough. The anger was still inside me, and it might bubble up at some point of time, resulting in some conflict. I had to release the emotion – anger! For that to happen, I needed to practice empathy. I needed to replace my negative thoughts about her with positive thoughts. I had to wish good things for her wholeheartedly. But this cannot happen overnight – it requires constant practice, and I decided to do it!

When I actively started making room for empathy, I felt myself softening and opening up. I started to put myself in her shoes and connect with her emotions. Why does she talk so much? Is it loneliness? Or is she having personal issues that she diverts in this manner? These three questions opened the door for me to give her my best wishes, as these are the situations where I could do some good for her. I don't need to talk to her on a personal level to do this. Now comes the tough part – practicing empathy!

Self-awareness and empathizing can solve most issues in a workplace environment, but it requires constant practicing.

How to Strike the Right Chord

Should I quit my job today? Do you wake up every single day asking this question to yourself? Are you the one taking the brunt of toxicity from your boss? I understand how it feels! Bosses who drain your energy with negativity are one good reason for you to quit your organization. But, what if you can learn to deal with such a toxic person? What if you make yourself less vulnerable to other such negative people in the future?

Yes, you can do it! Polishing your emotional intelligence skills will make you less interesting to those toxic people. You aren't their target anymore. Like bullying, you will no longer give them the desired result they are looking for. Make your current boss your tool to develop the skills that will make you less attractive and interesting to his toxic personality. There are several different strategies to deal with unreasonable bosses, irritating coworkers, etc. but we will look at the emotional parts of it to help find the best way to deal with the particular scenario or person.

Don't Rise to the Provocation

When the person is pushing your buttons, it is natural to burst out and react. It is impossible to fake the emotion that comes out. You will need to practice de-triggering yourself – this will help you take control of your emotions when the toxic person is trying to provoke you. When you are successful in dealing with the negativity of the person by de-triggering yourself, you feel empowered that you can move past a toxic relationship (which might help you in your personal life too). Sometimes, your team members who also suffer the brunt of toxicity can see you overcoming it and will feel the confidence to follow your example. It doesn't happen in an instant – you have to religiously practice de-triggering for some time, but once you get the hang of it, it comes to you naturally.

Support and Encourage

Support and encourage the others who are also a victim of such toxicity because, after a point, toxicity begins to feel normal. This can be dangerous. Talk to them passionately and remind them it is not normal – ask them to look at it as an opportunity to grow their emotional abilities. Encourage them to practice de-triggering, offer them opportunities to vent, but motivate them to turn that energy to balance the emotional intelligence factor.

Show Empathy

Empathize with your toxic boss – think of your boss as someone who is hurt and feel sorry for him, as he is harming his career path. When you do this, you begin to realize that the toxicity they are imposing on others is slowly eating them up. The moment you feel empowered – you see yourself as the one who can help them. But, don't overburden yourself in an attempt to fix them (because it is not in your hands – they will need to it themselves). Don't volunteer to go and talk to him. Carry the perception in your heart and wait for the opportunity to come to you. Grab it the moment you see it and share your perspective politely. They will soon begin to self-analyze.

Don't Be Judgmental

Before you criticize someone or judge their emotional intelligence, look in the mirror. Remember, when you judge someone, you are judging your conscience. When you throw criticism or judge a person, ask yourself – should I be doing this? Is it the real me? What does it say about my conscience?

If someone's EQ is triggering some part of you - before you react, think about why it's happening. Self-reflection exercises can help you comprehend your EQ. It will enlighten you on the areas you need to improve when it comes to your relationship with your colleague or boss. When you are dealing with people with a low EQ, you are testing your emotional intelligence. Ultimately, it is a two-way process.

Be an Example

Are you confident in your emotional intelligence? Do you believe it is an ongoing effort? If yes, you will have to look at every single interaction as an opportunity for yourself to model good emotional intelligence. We are humans and mistakes are part of our life. Instead of criticizing or judging another person (with low EQ), try to lead by example. Everyone reacts emotionally to certain situations at some point or the other. Self-reflection is the key factor for you to remember when you interact with a low EQ person. Put your EQ skills to work. Don't react when a co-worker frustrates you; rather give yourself time to think about it. Work on your thought process – what will happen if you react in a particular way? What will the consequences be? Will it affect the ambiance of the team? Will it strain your relationship with the person further? Think about the counter-arguments you will have to face when you react that way. When you self-reflect, your communication will be much clear, and you respond as effectively as you take into account the wants, feelings, opinions and thoughts of the opposite person.

Don't Assume, Ask

Some people might have a problem in communicating their concerns or problems effectively and this may be because of their low EQ. They don't realize that their stress and emotional reactions are responsible for triggering the opposite person. First and foremost, don't assume why the person acts in a particular way. Open the communication lines to diffuse the negative interactions you have with your boss or peers. Ask questions. Listen before you react. When you ask, you open a new framework of thought process. The boss or your colleague will understand that you are looking for a win-win situation that is beneficial for both.

Be Constructive in Your Feedback

When you open the communication line, you need to remember that you are walking down a two-way street. The best way to promote self-awareness and work on a relationship is by providing constructive feedback on other's behaviors. Constructive is just a word from the dictionary! If you have decided to share your observations about the person's behavior to them, ensure you do it in a polite, balanced and respectful manner. It can be anyone – your boss, peer or subordinate.

Let your feedback be precise and to the point – don't drag! If you are planning to talk to your colleague about a particular thing, be specific. For instance, you can tell your colleague that you weren't happy with the way you were interrupted during the presentation. But how do you put it across? Try it this way – *Yesterday during my presentation, you had interrupted me almost 5-6 times before even I could complete the point I was trying to make. It disturbed me, as I couldn't make my point. Why did you do so? Was there something in my presentation that needed improvement?* When you put it this way, you are conveying your emotions as well as giving them an opportunity to explain themselves. You are making them aware of their mistake and at the same time working on your emotional intelligence by trying to understand their thought process.

You will need to be at your best version every time – be it giving or receiving feedback. Be calm, listen in, give yourself time to take in what is being said, understand the message, take notes and be open about how you feel. Communication matters a lot! If the opposite person displays poor or vicious behavior, walk away calmly!

Emotionally Distance Yourself

If your attempts fail despite communicating or leading by example, the best way to deal with the person is by distancing yourself emotionally. Self-preservation is important! Yes, maintain your emotional distance from the person if it is someone whom you cannot avoid in the workplace.

Avoid taking things personally, as the accusations or outbursts are just a reflection of who they are. You need to distance yourself from them emotionally – this is crucial! You shouldn't let your dysfunctional boss affect your self-worth. Remember, you are worthy enough for yourself! There is no need to explicitly prove that to anyone – especially to someone who cannot recognize his or her emotional patterns.

Chapter Five: Actionable Tips and Strategies To Use EQ In Our Jobs

Having more people with high emotional intelligence in the workplace is good not just for the organization but the people around it too.

How do you assess your emotional intelligence? How will you know where you stand right now? Is there anything more you should do to work on your emotional quotient? There are many emotional intelligence tests available online to assess your EQ. It can tell you where you stand and also help you compare yourself against set benchmarks. The ISEI (Institute of Social and Emotional Intelligence) has some of the most effective emotional intelligence development tools and assessments.

Now that you have assessed your emotional intelligence skills, how do you use that in your workplace? How does your emotional intelligence manifest itself in the work environment? How do you recognize the emotional quotient in your colleagues at work?

EQ in Your Workplace

A few examples that can help you identify the emotional quotient in your workplace are:

Compassionate Ear

Not every day is a good day – some days are bad, sometimes even worse. Employees get upset, argue, have bad moods, get irritated – it's just one of those bad days! Dealing with such a situation says a lot about your emotional intelligence. How do you handle such employees? Do you pretend that it isn't happening? Do you criticize them? Do you snap at them, asking them to get over it?

Remember, one who is upset looks for a compassionate ear. Understanding and compassion is a major point when it comes to emotional intelligence. Being sentient to other's emotions and responding to them with empathy is important. It shows that every person does experience strong emotions and the feelings of each person matter.

But if some employees make it a practice to display negative emotions and almost follow it as a regular behavioral pattern, they will need to dedicated attention. It might mean that they have some deep-rooted issues, or they might require some form of counseling, or they might be attention-seekers.

More Listening, Less Talking

Have you been in a meeting where everyone does the talking? It may seem like they are all talking over each other, trying their best to get the last or loudest word. Ego and lack of respect for others seem to be the major issue here. It is essential for people to listen to each other before they respond – especially in meetings or conference calls. When people listen only to talk back, they are demonstrating a lack of emotional intelligence.

What is a good sign of emotional intelligence in such scenarios? People should listen and allow others to voice their opinion. This demonstrates mutual respect between the parties. This helps them to arrive at a constructive conclusion in conference calls or meetings.

Confidence to speak out openly

When people can express their thoughts openly, the air is filled with

EQ. Exchanging their viewpoints, speaking out their minds and openly expressing their emotions will mean emotional intelligence is demonstrated effectively. On the contrary, a workplace filled with employees who have bottled up emotions, opinions and thoughts are housing live ticking time bombs that can explode at any time.

People with high emotional intelligence don't get upset when opinions of others do not match with their own as long as the exchange of views is done with respect. They celebrate diversity, as they are open to new people and new ideas. They hold the opinion that people should be comfortable in expressing their thoughts more freely as they aren't machines.

Change is important

Change is unavoidable in the workplace. Change initiatives are common in most workplaces and the way the leadership team manages it says a lot about their management capabilities. When the employees accept change with an open mind, most change initiatives work. This tells a lot about the relationship between the employees and its top executive team.

If change is constantly resisted in an organization, it means there is a severe lack of understanding of the company's intention among the employees and vice-versa. Bringing emotional intelligence into the following areas will result in the successful introduction of new initiatives:

- Planning

- Introduction of the change initiative

- Response expected on the change

Flexibility

You will hear this word flexibility used more than often in the corporate field – it has become THE buzzword. The mandatory question for every candidate to answer in his or her selection process will be – Are you flexible? But how many organizations provide flexibility to their employees? Building flexibility in a way people can work happily and effectively is crucial as it is the only differentiating factor for them to retain their best talent from drifting out the door. Flexibility is important for today's generation, as the millennials have placed a high value on lifestyle.

Leaders with high emotional intelligence are quick enough to grab this concept and provide flexibility to their team members instead of being strict in imposing restrictions on how they are expected to work. These leaders can tune in with the changing demands and are ready to work with them in their style. They provide flexible work hours as long as they receive the intended and desired outcome from their team. They aren't too stringent when it comes to working hours, policies, working models, etc.

Creativity is the new style

When people are given the freedom to be creative, the leader can bring in innovative ideas for the benefit of the project and the team. Caging creativity is difficult as it a strong impulse, and it will find one way or the other to break free. Irrespective of the nature of your organization, creative people will always be respected and treated with importance regardless of the value your company places on creativity. Creative people and innovative organization make the best pair – creative people working in such a work environment are given the space, time and freedom to unleash their creativity and march ahead to achieve it.

Majority of working people would love to get social with their colleagues – the social impulse is always there. Getting social doesn't mean that you should get together after work for drinks every Friday – though it is a good idea some people wouldn't be interested, and it is bad to force them.

Social behavior doesn't come with a tagline – you don't always need to head to a pub to have fun. Traveling together with a colleague for work, chatting over the coffee vending machine, or eating lunch together or having a quick chat in the restroom are all signs of social behavior. When you are accompanied by one or more people to have fun and enjoy each other's company, you are getting into the social mode. This is the easiest way to de-stress yourself from a hectic work schedule or take a break from an irritating boss. Forming healthy and close bonds with your colleague need to be encouraged as it is a key element for a workplace that respects emotional intelligence.

These are just a few examples cited here, you can keep adding on to the list, and maybe your idea would be better than mine.

Tips to implement emotional intelligence at the workplace

Emotional Intelligence is relevant and crucial to life - be it for personal or professional growth. This one factor affects group performance, communication, group dynamics, motivation, individual performance and creativity in the workplace. The most important part of emotional intelligence is, it can reduce anxiety and protect one against stress (something which is quite common in a professional environment).

How can your emotional intelligence be measured? On what basis does the measuring happen? The emotional intelligence score depends on a series of abilities, and these can be grouped under four primary pillars:

- Self-awareness

- Self-management

- Social awareness

- Relationship management

Each of these pillars includes various emotional skills such as,

- Knowing your emotions (self-awareness)

- Managing your emotions and motivating yourself (self-management)

- Identifying and comprehending other people's emotions (social awareness)

- Managing the relationships and other's emotions (relationship management)

Working on these four pillars can help you improve your emotional intelligence thereby encouraging you to implement it in your workplace environment.

Self-awareness

"Knowing yourself is the beginning of all wisdom" – Aristotle

You can go through a series of different emotions in a day that can be a combination of positive emotions and negative emotions or either of them. Instead of letting the emotions control you, take a pause. Make a conscious effort to identify your feelings – how you feel and what you feel. Analyze – what is the cause of your emotions. Understand that emotions are short-lived and taking a decision based on them is mere foolishness. Take a deep breath when you are engulfed by negative emotions (frustration, fear, anger, apathy). Give time to yourself and think about how these emotions might affect you and your colleagues. Acknowledge the consequences of the behavior.

Self-management

"If you do not conquer self, you will be conquered by self" – Napoleon Hill

To avoid yourself from reacting hastily and responding inadequately, think of the different ways to control your emotions when you are at work. Don't respond or take decisions when you are facing a difficult situation especially when it is emotionally overwhelming. The most important thing is – you will need to accept both uncertainty and frustration, as they are part and parcel of any work environment. Deal with these feelings with a positive attitude. Doing so will help you increase your chances of finding suitable and relevant solutions for you, your colleagues as well as for the organization. Find out what you like best about your job, identify ways to find time to do things that motivate you but at the same time give in your full attention to the other tasks you aren't too keen in (as they are also part of your work responsibilities). Pat your back for every accomplishment you make – especially when you achieve your objective!

Social-awareness

"If you focus on results, you will never change. If you focus on change, you will get results" – Jack Dixon

Don't be judgmental and jump to conclusions. Always try to put yourself in other people's shoes and view the scenario. Listen more – active listening helps. Remember, how you treat others says a lot about yourself. Learn to empathize.

Relationship Management

"Your body communicates as well as your mouth. Don't contradict yourself." – Allen Ruddock.

Communication is the key to a good relationship. You should be able to put your thoughts into clear words and communicate with them effectively and neatly. Try to understand the person you are speaking to. All of us are different, so the way you interact or communicate with one person might not work well with another. Adapt according to the person or the scenario. Try to master the art of persuading others! Listen with rapt concentration, frame the right questions, put it across clearly, be specific with details – these simple tips should help you to learn the art of effective communication.

It cannot happen overnight – it is a long process, but regular practice will turn it into a habit that can be beneficial to you, both at a personal and professional level. The path is tough, and the road ahead is long, but it is worth the effort and time!

Motivation – the Driving Factor

Intrinsic motivation is a major component of emotional intelligence. It is the driving factor that helps achieve your goals. Self-motivation plays a major role when it comes to working toward a successful career. External motivational factors such as rewards, appreciation, etc. don't matter much, but it is the contentment and passion that keeps them going.

Approval, status and money – they are important; but for highly successful people, motivation doesn't come from these factors – it is much more than that. They love what they do, and they are passionate about it; they get fulfillment in doing them, they are committed to their work, they love challenges, they embrace change, and the enthusiasm they show towards their work is contagious. Giving up is not there in their dictionary – they push furthermore to overcome the obstacles and inspire others to work persistently to get to their goals.

But what do you do if you don't love your job? What if you are doing it only to keep your finances going? It can be difficult, but try out the following tips,

- You might not be passionate about your job, but there should be at least one thing that you like or love about your job. Focus on it!

- There can be things you hate about your job and the things you love about your job. Focus on the latter!

- Focus on the aspect you enjoy about your work and motivate yourself to work harder.

- You might love client interaction, which is a part of your job. Focus on it and improve your interpersonal and communication skills. Get your job done better and faster to impress your client. The appreciation mail from your customer will give you a sense of accomplishment. Feel it!

- Regardless of what it is, identify the components of the job that you like and take inspiration from them.

- A positive attitude will make you feel more energetic. Be optimistic in your workplace. This attitude will motivate and inspire not just you, but the others too.

Emotional intelligence is required not just for your wellness, but also for the success you are aiming at. You can learn more from emotion psychology to improve your emotional quotient and build more emotional competencies for a successful career and excellent work performance.

Social-Emotional Intelligence.

Social skills play a vital role when it comes to emotional intelligence – it is one area that helps you to manage and influence the emotions of other people effectively. This may sound like a big task, but it isn't really – a simple smile is enough. When you smile at a person, you are emitting positive vibrations that make him or her smile back at you. The positivity doesn't stop there – it spreads. Social skills - the final piece of the emotional intelligence jigsaw puzzle!

Emotional psychology research shows that people with high emotional intelligence have strong social skills, as they are skilled in identifying other people's emotions, respond to them based on the situation, and provide emotional support whenever required. These people are respected and valued at their workplace due to their effective communication skills and a positive attitude. Rapport building is an easy task for them as they are excellent team players. They can make effective leaders without the need to be pushed or trained.

How do you strengthen your social skills in the workplace?

- When you listen to what others have to say, do it actively. Passive listening doesn't help, and as when you listen without reacting, the speaker isn't motivated to continue with whatever he is trying to communicate.

- Active listening is important. Be attentive, ask the right questions and give feedback whenever required.

- This will show your team that you are indeed interested in what the others have to say, you are passionate about your project, and that you are ready to work with others to help achieve a shared goal.

- Focus on the signals people send through their body language and cues. These gestures will tell you a lot about what they're thinking. Nonverbal communication is the key to recognizing other's emotions.

- Sharpen your persuasion skills. When you can make your colleagues and boss listen to your ideas, you are taking the first step to influence them. Clarity in communication does the rest of the job.

- Never get involved in any office drama, but at the same time ensure you can manage the conflict.

- You don't need petty office politics eating at your head. You may not always be able to avoid conflicts, but focus on what others are saying and find ways to resolve issues, thereby minimizing the tensions.

Chapter Six: How Emotional Intelligence Can Really Help Out In Relationships

Have you ever made a snarky comment to your boss in a moment of anger during a heated discussion? Did you ever have a fiery argument with your spouse about a small issue blew up into something huge? Have you ever regretted making an important decision when you were upset? Don't feel bad if the answer is yes! All of us have gone through this. Why does this happen? When you are unable to recognize and understand your emotions, you are controlled by them and react hastily. These are all problems of poor or low emotional intelligence.

People with high emotional intelligence are associated with the following:

- Increased creativity

- Change acceptance

- Good team worker

- Excellent work performance

- Retention at work

All of these are linked to a professional career. The best part is, people who do well in their career enjoy better interpersonal relationships at home. Dr. Nicola Schutte conducted a study in the early 2000s with her team where she was able to show that people who believed their partners to be emotionally intelligent were highly satisfied with their marital relationship and expected more satisfaction in the future.

Emotionally intelligent people can understand four crucial, critical things:

- They can understand other's emotions, as they are smart in recognizing them. This particular skill is extremely tough when you are dealing with people who aren't emotionally open. You can easily identify that someone is sad when they are crying, but how do you understand the grief in the person if he or she is trying to hide it? People with high EQ can do it, and if you practice EQ, you can do it too.

- They are aware of their own emotions and feelings. They are always in touch with their emotions and know what they feel, how they feel and why they feel. They don't push away the emotions by brushing it aside or giving it a wrong label. Regulating emotions is key, as there is a difference between showing your frustration during an official meeting or waiting for the meeting to finish to show your irritation. Consequences for the former can be dangerous and even spoil your relationship with your boss, while the latter gives you time to think over it so that you put it across in a much better way.

- Thoughts create emotions! Emotionally intelligent people understand this and work towards clearing and controlling the thought. Doing this can decrease the power of your emotions. Sometimes, your thinking process is affected by your feelings and mood, i.e., over-thinking. For example, your decision-making skills will begin to waver when you are upset, but when you are calm, you make decisions that handle the conflict much better.

- These people understand the correlation between their actions and the emotional reactions it can cause in other people. For instance, an emotionally intelligent man will know that breaking the promise he made to his wife can result in her feeling hurt.

Building emotional intelligence is a great way to improve your relationship with others – it can be a tough task, but it is doable. How do you build your emotional intelligence? There are many ways to do so, but we will look at the easiest and practical way.

- Observe your thought process.

- Watch the way your thoughts connect with your emotions throughout the day.

- The chemicals released in your brain will change the way you feel about things.

- Thoughts release these chemicals.

- Notice the connection between your thoughts and emotions.

- Work on decreasing negative emotions by not giving the power to the thoughts that create those emotions.

- Focus on increasing your thoughts towards positive emotions.

You will need to find out ways to calm you down. Going for a run? Walking around the block for few minutes? Making a call to a friend? Doing some yoga postures? Closing your eyes and clearing your head for 5 minutes? Hugging your pet? Watching funny videos of your kid? Find out what works best for you and put it into practice.

If you are going to be in the vicinity of a negative person whom you are trying to avoid, focus on the positives that might come out of the conversation before you speak to him or her.

How To Determine Whether My Emotional Intelligence Needs Improvement

The act of loving someone calls for emotional intelligence – yes, you read it right! You require emotional intelligence to love, as you need to empathize, recognize problems and should be able to connect with the person on a much deeper level. The way you solve issues at home and your choice of partner indicates a lot about the connection between emotional intelligence and love. When you can harness the power of emotional intelligence successfully, you tend to see an improvement in your relationships.

The conflicts that occur in your relationships mostly rely on your emotional intelligence, which is the ability to observe, identify and respond appropriately to the emotions. Individuals with high emotional intelligence are better at processing their feelings and that of their partners healthily. Emotional intelligence plays a major role in romantic relationships – your EQ can influence whom you fall in love with and how the relationship will play out over a period of time. A series of failed relationships or having a hard time connecting with people (in general) will mean that your emotional quotient needs improvement.

The following are some of the classic signs that will tell you that you need to boost your emotional intelligence.

- Bursting into laughter or lashing out in anger in a moment signals your lack of emotional quotient. This is because you are finding it difficult to control your emotions.

- Having a tough time in building and maintaining healthy relationships with colleagues and friends may indicate your problems with emotional intelligence. Lack of social skills.

- Are you finding it difficult to sympathize or empathize? If you want to have a lasting relationship, you should be able to empathize with the feelings of others. It is an essential part of a healthy relationship.

- You have an issue with your emotional quotient if you are unable to connect with media, movies or books. Tragedy, comedy and horror – all these genres are meant to stimulate your emotions, but if media, movies or books don't move you, there is something wrong with your emotional intelligence.

It is crucial to understand that emotional intelligence plays a major role in every part of your life – it helps dictate a range of things, from a successful career to a contented personal relationship. For some people, emotional intelligence is naturally high while for some it is low. If you feel you have low EQ, don't hesitate to take steps to work on improving it. Self-improvement is a necessity in everything! Mindfulness is the basis for emotions – try meditating or getting into yoga sessions to improve your mindfulness.

The following simple steps will help you work towards improving your emotional quotient:

- Practice self-control. Pause, breathe (deep breath), count (for few seconds) and compose (think) a response. Don't react immediately.

- Abstain. If you are the one who responds indifferently to situations or makes inept jokes, give yourself time to listen to the opposite person before you frame a response. For example, making jokes at a funeral or other tragedy to lighten the grief.

You have so many different ways to improve your emotional intelligence. Choose the best and work on it!

Strategies to Improve Emotional Intelligence

How do I set things right with my partner? Why do I make a big issue of small things that spoil my relationship with my husband? Why am I unable to control my anger when she points out my negatives? Why do I get frustrated with my kids when they go overboard - after all, they're just kids?

These are few of the many questions that keep popping up in your mind whenever you're upset about your strained relationship or your inability to control your emotions. How do you work on it? We will look at a few strategies to develop the emotional quotient for better and healthy relationships.

- Observe your reactions to people. Do you jump to conclusions? Are you judgmental? Do you stereotype people? Look at yourself. Be honest with yourself. Question how you think and interact with people. Be open-minded. Accept their version. Look at their needs and perspectives.

- Think about how you behave in your workplace. Are you an attention seeker? Do you look for an opportunity to shine, and grab it the moment you see it? Don't be bothered too much about praise. Shift your focus towards others. Offer them a chance to shine.

- Self-evaluate. Do you accept that you are not perfect? Will you accept negative feedbacks on your behavior? What are your weaknesses? Are you willing to work on certain areas to make yourself better?

- Study the way you react to stress. How do you react during a stressful situation? What are the series of emotions you go through? Do you easily become upset when things don't turn

66

out the way you want them to? Do you look for a chance to blame others even when they are not at fault? Do you always keep bubbling with anger? You will need to keep your emotions under control when things don't work in your favor. Staying calm and composed in a difficult situation is highly valued not just in the professional world, but also in a personal life.

- You are responsible for your actions. Take responsibility. If you hurt someone's feelings, don't hesitate to apologize. Do it directly. Don't avoid the person or ignore what you did. When you make an honest attempt to set things right, people will be more than willing to forgive and forget. They feel happy when you apologize. They respect you when you accept your mistake.

Emotional intelligence is necessary to turn your intentions into action. If you want to make important decisions on things that matter to you the most, you must do it with utmost care. Connect with people, nurture your feelings, react after thinking and most important of all, empathize!

Chapter Seven: Getting The Ship Up And Running Through These Powerful EQ Ways

The one question you (or anyone for that matter) cannot honestly deny is:

Have you ever said or done something when you were so overwhelmed by your emotions that you regretted it instantly?

The truth is, it is possible to learn to handle your emotions in a more constructive manner, and this ultimately means working on improving your emotional intelligence. The concept of emotional intelligence is becoming popular in contemporary psychology and for all the good reasons. Emotional intelligence is not just linked to healthy and successful personal relationships, but is also coupled with an increased ability to handle stress and improved work performance.

So, if you want to have a deeper connection with your romantic partner, colleagues or friends, your top priority should be to cultivate your emotional intelligence.

Secrets for Developing High Emotional Intelligence

Awareness (both self and social) is the starting point for high emotional intelligence. When you can recognize your own emotions and the impact it can have on you and others, your self-awareness is going well. Understanding your emotions is the first step and the moment you can do that, you become thoughtful enough to recognize other people's emotions too. Apart from identifying their emotions, you are also able to gauge the impact it can have on the person and the scenario.

How is it possible to create this awareness? It begins with reflection – self-reflection! You question yourself and try to find the answers to know who you are.

- What are my strengths?

- What are my weaknesses?

- How much do my emotions affect my normal routine?

- Are my decision-making skills and thought processes affected depending on my mood?

- What is going on within me that influences what others do or say?

- What sort of feelings do I get when I am confronted?

When you ponder such questions, you are more likely to gain valuable insights that can be useful to work on your emotional quotient.

Take a moment to stop and think before you act or speak – it's easy in theory but difficult to practice. However, taking serious steps to practice the act of pausing can save you from making hasty decisions or getting yourself into embarrassing situations. Simply put, pausing for a moment abstains you from making any permanent decision based on a momentary emotion. It is true that you have very little control over the emotions you experience in a split second. However, the reaction to the said emotions is absolutely in your control, and you can harness it by driving your thoughts in the right direction. You might not control all the situations and their outcome, but your attitude can be controlled! When you work on controlling your thoughts, you are working in advance to refuse to give in to your emotions. You brave it and deny becoming its slave! This way, you are working in harmony with your values and goals.

Feedback on your behavior and attitude is important, but what if you are receiving negative feedback? How do you learn to handle your criticism? Do you take the positive side of it? Or do you succumb to your emotions again? It is true that negative feedback can be discouraging or de-motivating, but you need to remember that it is a chance to learn. Some people can present negative feedback in a positive and constructive manner, but most of them are pretty straight and blunt. Remember to work on your flaws even when the feedback is not presented to you in a 'nice' way. Even if you're subjected to baseless criticism, respond, don't react. One good thing about this is that you get to know what people think of you. Ask yourself – How can I work towards a better version of me – a more positive version?

And you don't always need to be an open book – there is no need to share all your thoughts and secrets with everyone. Being genuine is fine, but authenticity has a different meaning to it. It means sticking to your principles and values and saying what you mean the way you mean. Not everyone will appreciate your feelings and thought process, but the ones who matter the most to you will do!

Empathy – the basis of any relationship! When you can understand other people's feeling and thoughts, you are in a better position to emotionally connect with them. Don't label or judge people! Work yourself in a way where you can see things from their perspective. Give them the benefit of the doubt! You don't necessarily need to agree with everything they have to say or mean, but you can merely work towards understanding their viewpoint. This way you get to build better and deeper connections! This helps with a deeper and more intimate relationship with your partner.

Appreciation and acknowledgment are two things every human being longs for! When you are appreciated, you feel happy and motivated to do things. Similarly, when you are acknowledged, you gain the feeling of being heard. You satisfy this particular craving in people when you praise them or acknowledge them – this helps build their trust. How do you do this? It all begins when you focus on the good in the opposite person. You inspire him or her to become a better version of who they are when you openly appreciate them. Reframing negative feedbacks constructively can make your partner or friend or family realize that you are in a way trying to help them create a better version of themselves. They will not look at you as a criticizer but would be happy to hear what you have to say!

The most important thing of all is – accepting your mistake and apologizing when you are wrong. It takes a lot of guts to accept your mistake and say the word sorry. But when you do so from your heart, you are naturally attracting the other person to you, as you are becoming humble in the process. Sometimes - especially in a romantic relationship - apologizing can make a huge difference. It doesn't always mean that you're wrong when you say sorry. It means that you value your relationship more than your ego!

Grudges can kill you from inside! Holding on to the past or hanging on to resentment is like stabbing yourself with a knife and expecting the other person to bleed. The person who was responsible for this would have moved on with his or her life, but you cling on to it, refusing to give yourself a chance to heal. Forgiving and forgetting is not easy, but when you try to forgive and forget, you open the lock of your cage. You don't allow your emotions to hold you hostage anymore and you start moving on in life.

It has become so common nowadays for people to break a promise whenever they feel like doing so. When you commit something, you are responsible for making sure you adhere to it. Imagine a scenario where you committed to spending time with your friend at a movie but didn't do so. On the same day, you had a major deadline to meet, and you had also promised to take your kid on a picnic, but none of this happened. Who do you think will be affected more? Bailing out on your friend will cause little harm to him when compared to your kid and business deadline. The problem is, when you don't keep your word – be it big or small - and make it a habit of it, then you naturally start losing the trust people have in you. Trustworthiness and reliability come only when you adhere to your commitment.

Do you know the best way to impact the emotions of your loved ones positively? It's pretty simple – help them. Not everyone cares about your educational background or financial status, or the position you hold in the society. But what matters is how helpful you are – how willing you are to take time out of your busy schedule to listen to other's issues or help them out when needed. If you're ready to get into the pit and work along with them, that's all that matters! When you go out of your way to help others, you inspire the people around you and build the trust. The inspiration will make them follow your lead, and you spread positivity this way.

All said and done, and you also need to realize that there is a negative side to emotional intelligence. What happens when certain people try to manipulate other's emotions for a selfish cause or maybe to endorse a personal agenda? How do you handle such situations? The only way is by sharpening your emotional intelligence. You need to do this to protect yourself when you are surrounded by such individuals.

Improving Relationships Through Emotional Intelligence

Since you were born, you start building relationships – a skill you learn with experience. How do you ensure the relationships you build are healthy? When you refine your approach and build on your skills, you begin to adapt to people's needs as well as your own. What is the starting point to build a relationship? Interaction! The way you interact with a person builds a base to your relationship. You come across so many people in your life, and you interact with many of them – some of the interactions are short-lived, while some are meaningful and deep.

One way to use your emotional intelligence is by building healthy interpersonal relationships. How do you build a healthy relationship? Mutual understanding! When both parties can understand each other – the thoughts, emotions, nonverbal cues, etc. the relationship becomes healthy. For this to happen, you should learn to empathize, accept the other person's values and ethics, and most important of all – trust! Conflicts and disagreements are bound to happen as they are unavoidable but what matters is how you deal with these issues. This is where understanding and learning comes into the picture. It's not the conflict that matters, but how you managed the conflict and ensured your relationship didn't become strained.

How can you be successful in your relationship? When you are constantly working on creating a healthy connection with people, you are spreading positivity. A successful relationship can result in a successful life – a life filled with love, joy, contentment and tranquility. However, most people are good when they start a relationship, but when the connection grows, they find it extremely difficult to keep it intact and healthy. With time, the relationship weakens and fails.

When you build a relationship, you need to nurture the connection you make, the bond you create with the utmost care. Treat it like a fragile plant or a newborn baby that needs care and protection. The main reason couples fall apart is the lack of emotional intelligence both parties display. You create an intimate connection or bond while building relationships when you know how to manifest proper emotional intelligence.

There are five important skills that you need to apply to build and maintain a healthy relationship. When you do this, you apply your emotional intelligence in the right way to nurture the relationship.

Manage Stress

Today, stress has become a normal part of life and handling this demon in the right way not only helps you maintain a relationship, but also your health. Negative stress weakens your emotions and doesn't allow you to think straight. Balanced thinking isn't possible when emotions start controlling you. You need to identify your stress levels when they spiral out of control, and this is crucial. Managing stressful situations before they ruin your relationship saves not only you, but also your partner from emotional imbalance.

Recognize and Handle Emotions

You will need to identify and manage your emotions before they get out of control. Your emotions are affected by the daily encounters you have with different people and your own life experiences. For your communication to be clear and effective, you need to:

- Take control of your emotions

- Learn to identify them

- Understand how they can affect your actions

- Comprehend the effect they can have on your relationships with others.

You can understand your needs and goals when you are aware of your emotional quotient.

Nonverbal Communication

Learning and improving your nonverbal communication is important as this communication type has more power than words. 99 percent of the time, your thoughts and emotions are conveyed through your body language, even if you don't mean to. It is so evident, and unless you have control over your emotions, you are bound to be defeated by your body signals. If you want to maintain a healthy and strong relationship, make sure you communicate well through the proper use of:

- Eye contact

- Facial expressions

- Voice

- Body movements

- Gestures

When you are saying something, mean it! Make eye contact. Hug your partner often. Sometimes a sincere hug means more than a million words!

Good Humor

When you can use humor and play in a relationship, you succeed in turning a serious situation into a light one. Good humor can turn an upsetting situation in a relationship to a relaxing one. It gives both partners a feeling of relief, as you don't end up yelling at each other. You should be able to sort out your differences through playfulness and humor. This will make sure all your relationship problems aren't taken seriously but handled appropriately.

Resolving Conflict

Conflicts are so common when it comes to a relationship – especially with the relationship you have with your spouse or partner. When you can healthily resolve the conflicts, you are working toward a healthy and long-lasting relationship. Not all relationships are smooth – be it professional or personal! Display your emotional intelligence by responding properly during disagreements or disputes with your partner. Don't react and don't overreact! Healthily manage your conflicts – listen and then talk!

Chapter Eight: What Has This Got To Do With Emotional Intelligence?

Self-awareness. Your journey in increasing your emotional quotient begins when you enhance your self-awareness ability. Simply put, you need to be aware of your own emotions before you manage them effectively. When you are aware of your emotions, you can empathize naturally, which will help you understand what others are going through. People who have high emotional self-awareness will know how they feel at any given point of time, what caused the feeling (the source) and can also identify the physical symptoms (such as headaches, sweaty palms, shivering hands, etc.) related to those feelings.

How do you start with self-awareness?

The following three steps are the best way to start with the self-awareness process:

Assess your state of emotions

First, you need to check in with yourself and analyze your emotional state. Dedicate time to reading your emotions during the day. Question yourself and ensure you answer them truthfully. Start firing questions at yourself:

- What is that I am feeling?

- Why do I feel this way?

- Is there a source?

- How are these particular feelings affecting my body?

- Are they manifesting themselves positively or negatively?

- Do I feel tension in my body parts, like feeling worn out, anxious, scared, elation or clenched teeth?

Give a name to your emotions

Learn to label your emotions when you can determine what you feel and how you feel. This can help identify the source of the negative feelings – the trigger point of your emotions. Examples of labeling your emotions – surprise, anger, fear, passion, etc. Write down the labels for your emotions along with the thoughts that triggered these particular emotions. For instance, if anger is the label of your emotion, the trigger to this negative emotion might be – provocation by someone you don't like, a body gesture that angered you, etc.

When you can identify the source of the emotion and the corresponding feeling, you see it written on the paper. It becomes clear to you what you need to do to improve your response to that particular trigger.

Listen to your emotions

Be in the moment and pay attention to what your emotions and feelings are trying to tell you at any precise moment. This particular information can then be used to gain additional guidance and insight from within to work on the problem or issue.

Self-Awareness and Its Role in Emotional Intelligence

You're sitting in your cubicle and reviewing your client accounts. You are analyzing the profits each client has given for the month, and it looks good to you. Though you don't sense any strong feelings, you know you are feeling composed and satisfied. You hear your phone ring, and you pick it up. The angry voice of the client reverberates, and suddenly you feel the panic rising within you. The client is one of your biggest accounts that generates a substantial profit for you every month. He is threatening to withdraw the project and give it to another company as your team has missed the deadline. In an instant, you realize that you are no longer composed as you can feel your heartbeat rising. Your hands sweat and your breathing becomes intense – you realize you are getting anxious.

This is how you become aware of your emotions and self-awareness is a simple phrase used for an intricate set of emotions. The awareness of yourself on various levels is referred to as self-awareness. It can be your body and its physical reactions, your intentions, your emotions, your inferences, your values, your goals and your knowledge about how you come across as a person to others. When you have more self-awareness, you can adjust the responses to others easily. This ultimately results in mutually satisfying transactions and interactions.

Tune in to yourself and become aware of what you are going through as you experience the emotion. This way you can enhance your emotional intelligence. The energy from your body at the cellular level composes all your emotions. They are a form of data. Both positive and negative emotions provide you with information that can help you assess the situation or scenario at that particular time. Learning to tune in to these messages they send you can help you become more emotionally healthy.

Feel Your Feelings

When I keep repeating the phrase be aware of your emotions, it doesn't mean express it. You merely need to feel what you are feeling – expressing the emotion is your choice. You can make a conscious choice on how to respond to your feelings or maybe don't respond at all! But you can make all these choices only if you're aware of your emotions. You need to know what you are experiencing. Being aware of your emotions will open up new alternatives for your behavior. Your responses to your emotions will be instantaneous if you aren't aware of what is happening within you. The responses to your emotions will not be guided by an insight or reasoning.

For instance, if you are starting your day with a negative experience (maybe you argued with your co-passenger in the train on the way to work), it can leave you frustrated and irritated throughout the day. This will affect the interactions you have with your team or other people that you wouldn't even be aware of. When someone points out your negative behavior (irritation or frustration), you are surprised into awareness.

The moment you figure out what you are experiencing, you feed this information to your brain, which thinks about the emotion and helps you make a more conscious effort to change that negative into positive. Poor self-awareness can get you into trouble when someone pushes your trigger button. You suddenly find yourself blowing a simple thing out of proportion. Why does this happen? It's because your limbic memory is triggered. What does this mean? Sometimes you bring back the responses you learned during your childhood. For instance, you might unknowingly get into a defensive crouch when your boss or partner is yelling at you. Why? Because your limbic memory brought back an old remembrance of verbal abuse you experienced in your childhood.

This is why you need to be aware of your emotions – being self-aware is the solution to control yourself and act freely as recited by your conscious mind. This can give you true relationships, and you cultivate the habit of showing empathy to people around you. The problem is that you're unaware of your feelings until the moment they come out strong. However, the undeniable fact is that the human brain keeps thinking something or the other, which naturally leads to some feeling. The feeling is always there just that you are unaware until it gets stronger.

Like how experts say – you need to pay more attention to your cognitive process to grow intelligent (intellectual intelligence). Similarly, you need to pay more attention to what you feel and why you feel it to become emotionally intelligent. Self-awareness begins when you tune in to your physical self. People who have suffered severe physical or mental trauma can find it difficult to be aware of what is happening to their inner self. They become emotionally handicapped. It turns off their awareness ability, which might cripple their other abilities or leadership potential at the workplace.

How can the damage be rectified? A positive relationship, therapy and the willingness to change can make things right! Science proves that adult brains can relearn the patterns of emotions through patience and perseverance.

Language to Describe Your Emotions

What is the language you use to describe your feelings? Unfortunately, not many people can label their feelings beyond the basic ones such as worry, pain, anger, joy or hurt. The irony here is we usually remember all the negative emotions but forget the positive emotions quickly. Self-awareness is critical when it comes to emotional intelligence. When you are in touch with what you feel, you take steps in being aware of your emotional patterns. It is critical!

Now, it is time to use a language to describe your emotions. You should be able to comfortably describe what you feel with words or through body language. Emotions are energies that can motivate you or withdraw from you. When your emotions expand, it gives you a push to do things, but when it contracts, it pulls you back.

How do emotions reveal themselves?

When you aren't taking the time to listen to your feelings, label them or deal with them through effective communication, they will manifest in the body. Your health will deteriorate, you'll find it difficult to concentrate on things, you'll feel pain in certain parts of your body and tiredness will be your constant companion. When you focus on your emotions and feel them gradually, they will intensify, helping you to learn and connect.

Suppressing your emotions – be them negative or positive – isn't good for your health, as you deny your brain access to important natural chemicals. To handle your emotional weakness, you use alternatives such as drugs, alcohol or medicine, but they are poor substitutes for your natural brain chemicals. Expressing emotions is required as it is healthy for your brain and body.

Getting in Tune With Your Emotions

You will need to learn and follow the path to self-awareness for success and personal growth. As Daniel Goleman rightly said, the keystone of emotional intelligence is being self-aware. You need to be in tune with your emotions. Don't cage yourself in your mind! Free yourself and feel the freedom you deserve! How do you start?

Learn about yourself, as this will help you understand which area needs to be worked on. The process of understanding yourself is the first step to becoming self-aware. When you can identify the emotions that you experience, comprehend the feelings linked to the emotion, understand your thought pattern and respond accordingly, you are becoming increasingly aware of your emotions. Emotional awareness is an exercise everyone needs to follow.

Intensive training is given on emotional awareness to professional sportsmen and sportswomen, as they need to be aware of their emotions and overcome them during the game. They should not be letting their anger or frustration affect their performance during the game.

You will be more confident about what you can do and what you cannot do when you are aware of your emotional strengths and limits. Your confidence will make you more positive and certain about what you believe to be right. Assertiveness doesn't mean that you always get what you want the way you want. It is more to do with the way you put across your ideas and thoughts confidently. This self-confidence will make you justify why you believe a particular idea or decision is right! The following competencies are linked to self-awareness:

- Perfect self-assessment (recognizing your limitations and your strengths)

- Self-confidence (Knowing your capabilities and self-worth)

- Self-awareness of your emotions (Identifying your emotions and understanding the impact they can have on your life)

Self-awareness and emotional self-awareness can be developed through practice. All you need to do is spend time on yourself. Recognize the areas that need development. Make a conscious effort to work on those areas. Develop and strengthen that particular aspect of yourself.

How do you become aware of your strengths? How do you identify the areas you need to improve? Ask yourself the following questions:

- What are your strengths? Rate yourself based on your strengths you identified.

- Are you open to receiving feedback? Ask people for feedbacks. Keep an open mind and listen to what others have to say about you. This will help you know what they think about you

- Have you taken an online assessment test? Take a formal, emotional awareness assessment test. Try a series of different tests. It'll be fun – personality test, skill test, discovering your abilities, your values, etc.

Do either of the three that are mentioned above, or maybe do all the three for best results!

Improving Self-Awareness

Look into you. Talk to your inner self. The outside world has bombarded you with so many messages that you often fail to communicate with the world that is within you. Self-awareness is all about getting back in touch with your inner self. Know who you are! Practice by following some exercises that will help you understand who you are.

- Start writing a journal. Ask specific questions to yourself and try finding honest answers to them. What are the things that are of utmost importance to me? Write on this topic. Evaluate and comprehend your thoughts, feelings and emotions as you write. It might even take days for you to finish writing this. Once you are done, read it for yourself. Then ask the next crucial question, am I spending my time on what is important to me?

- Think about your work and the way you do it. Is your work or at least some part of your work related to your passion? Do you like what you do? Don't just take on any project; instead, try to be part of activities that engage your heart and mind in unison. For instance, your job area might be developing a software – go one step ahead and take additional responsibility by interacting with the client directly (especially if you are someone who loves to build a relationship). This will help you to work better to satisfy your client – specifically when you are the one who is directly interacting. What if you don't know what you love? What if you don't know what you are passionate about? That means you've lost in touch with yourself completely. You need to rekindle the relationship with yourself. Get back to the journal – write down what you used to love when you were a child or maybe in the recent past.

- When you start working on being aware of your emotions, you naturally begin to become aware of your physical body. Listen to your body and find out where you are feeling a reaction to your emotion. For instance, some may feel uneasiness in the neck and shoulder area when they are tense. For some, an uncomfortable feeling is experienced in the abdominal area when they are upset. For some, a severe headache means frustration or anger. Pain in the jaws and chest indicates bottled up negative emotions. The intensity of your emotion can turn into energy that shows in your body, but you shouldn't be letting it control you.

- Self-curiosity is good, especially when you develop curiosity in observing self. Imagine yourself to be the third person – an outsider - and then think about your thought process. Switch off autopilot mode and start tuning it to yourself. Dwell on the emotional extremes of your consciousness. Identify your loud and subtle moods. Be curious as to why you feel certain emotions in a said pattern. Observe the pattern and work on improving it more positively.

- Spend at least 15 minutes regularly working on building your awareness. Do a self-reflection exercise. Do this at peace and don't allow other stuff to interfere during this process. How do you do it? Relax and do something pleasant and silent. For instance, close your eyes and listen to your favorite instrumental. Let your thoughts wander at their will. Don't control them. Just go with the flow.

- When you are traveling to work, think about two different situations that you might mostly come across during the day. Let one be something that doesn't produce a strong emotion while the other results in some form of emotion. When you think about it, you are living the experience of the situation. Pay attention to the emotions you come across at the thought of those scenarios. What is your reaction? What is happening in your head? Do you feel something going on in your body? Write this down in a small notepad and keep it at your desk. Follow this for 10-15 days and write down how you feel in each of these areas when you relate to a particular situation:

    - Breathing (intense or relaxed)

    - Feelings (intensity and what you feel)

    - Heart rate (normal or rapid)

    - Situation (write down the situation)

    - Muscle tightness (do you experience tightness in any area of your body? If so, write it down)

    - Perspiration (do you sweat?)

- Fix yourself when you feel low energy or sense tension in your physical body. Move from your current place and get some fresh air. Drink cold water. Eat a healthy snack. Go out and stare at something scenic – a plant or flower or bushes or anything green. Get up and stretch yourself. Relax your muscles and shrug your shoulders, or maybe do a twist. If you want your energy level to be high the whole day, you need to give yourself a three-minute break every 30 minutes.

- When you work on improving your self-awareness, you naturally become aware of both your good and bad stuff. You get to know about certain things that you don't like about yourself. Acknowledge it and accept the fact that no man or woman is wise or powerful enough to get rid of all the flaws. Problems are normal, but when you are aware of them, you can turn them into a challenge, which will give you an opportunity to grow. How do you do it?

  - Identify your problem areas and define them carefully. Ask yourself – what am I doing here? What is going on here?

  - Brainstorm! Write down all the ideas and suggestions that come to your mind as a solution to your problems. Even if they are the silliest ones – write it down.

  - Evaluate the pros and cons of the suggestions/ideas you had written down. Try to maintain a balance between your heart and brain! Is your gut instinct telling you something? Follow that! Will you be able to commit to working on the solution with your heart and soul?

  - Ponder that solution. Live with it and give it some

time. Don't jump into trying it. Follow your gut instinct. Listen to what it has to say. Develop your plan accordingly. After a couple of days, if you still feel committed with all your heart and head, it is time for action.

- Take action and evaluate how it is going to be implemented. Modify only when needed. Work on it and see yourself improving!

Request feedback from people around you! I know I keep repeating it, but receiving feedback is the best way to know if you are on the right track. Self-awareness doesn't come from self-observation alone – it also includes the observation of people around you. When I mean people around you, not the random people or strangers – it should come from your loved ones, your friends, your peers, your boss! Their feedback and comments can be valuable to improve your self-awareness.

This is the reason why most organizations use 360-degree feedback for their employees – they get feedback from their peers, customers, subordinates and bosses. This is a performance review system used by the employers to acquire significant data and information by seeking feedback from people. This is the best way to reduce the blind spots and increase your awareness.

Going out of your way to improve self-awareness

Receive feedback from trusted colleagues and close friends. They're the ones who know you and observe you – they can help you see how you come across to other people.

- Talk to a friend or colleague who is brutally honest with you. He or she should listen to you and at the same time be open with the feedback. You should be able to talk to this person regularly to know how you are perceived by others. Ask them to help you look at yourself objectively. Talk about how focused you are on your purpose and if it needs improvement or change in plans. They should act as an honest advisor who can help you both personally and professionally. This can improve not only your career but also your health.

- Ask them to point out the flaws in you – especially the destructive patterns they see in you. For instance, if you are sarcastic or demanding or cynical when you meet new challenges, it will reflect directly on your behavior, and your advisor can point it out easily. If you need to control them, you need to be aware of these patterns. Get your journal back, start noticing these patterns in you and write them down. Find out the causes or sources or trigger points for these patterns. Keep a log of what happens when this behavior occurs.

- The best way to enhance your self-awareness is by making your trusted colleague your partner in this process. Have lunch together and discuss it with the person regularly. Exchange the information and observations on the behavior – let her talk about your behavior, and you talk about hers! Take turns in sitting on the hot seat.

- Most importantly – ask them to be honest about what they think of you. What is their perception of you? Don't hesitate to do this! There is no need to feel scared or threatened in thinking about what they might say. Whatever it is, face it and acknowledge it! Look at it as an opportunity to work on yourself. This will help in increasing your self-reflection, self-knowledge and self-awareness. If you are nervous thinking about they may say, take deep breaths and listen with an open mind! This could be what is needed for that special breakthrough and try not to let ego or fear come into play at this juncture. An open mind, a really open one, would be really helpful at this moment. It helps to cope with whatever feedback that is going to come, and also with whatever potential feelings of uncomfortableness being generated.

Chapter Nine: Getting To The Root of It All

Emotions are the driving force for moving forward in life. They can make you or break you! They can take you on a series of a roller-coaster rides on a day when you thought you are steady and stable. Confused? Do you want to know the series of emotions you go through in a single day?

You wake up as usual, but you're slightly tense as you have an important presentation today, for which you had prepared for weeks. You reach the office and log in to check your email. You've been notified that the presentation has been canceled; you feel irritated as you had spent a significant period of time preparing for it. But then you get a call from a friend who wants you to come over for a get-together dinner sometime that week, and you feel happy and positive. You go on with your day's work, and it is time for lunch. You realize that you forgot to pack your lunch, so you head to the food court area and find a long queue. You feel frustrated and annoyed as your stomach is growling in hunger. You see your team member in the queue and smile at him. He offers to get you lunch as he is already in the queue. You feel relaxed. Back in your cubicle, you are seriously working on a document when a coworker comes to you with an issue, and you feel interrupted. Later, you get a call from your sister who hasn't contacted with you in ages. You become serious, as you think she wouldn't be calling unless it was something important. She tells you that she is separating from her husband; you are shocked and feel sad for her. Then, you receive a call from your CEO who informs you about the incentives that are going to be released for the quarter, and you feel excited and proud as the CEO has directly called you. In the evening, a colleague brags about her exciting holiday plans, and you feel jealous as you realize you are exhausted and need a break too. You leave the office and pick up your kids on the way back home. They surprise you with a Mother's Day greeting card that they made; you feel loved. You get the dinner ready for your family and put your kids to bed. You finally feel relieved that the day has ended.

Are you familiar with this scenario? Yes, it is the routine of almost everyone. In one day, you go through a series of emotions, but most of the time you don't dwell in the emotions for too long. However, certain emotions might keep lingering in your mind, obstructing your thought patterns, distracting your decisions, affecting your behavior and energy. This emotional roller-coaster ride is what is labeled as life – we are mere puppets waiting for the next course of action to take place based on the emotional change that is to happen. It isn't fair! You shouldn't be controlled by your emotions; rather, you should have some sort of tool to help take control of them.

"I don't want to be at the mercy of my emotions. I want to use them, to enjoy them, and to dominate them." – Oscar Wilde

As Oscar Wilde says, you need to know how to navigate your emotions to make the best out of your life. Your emotional health is more important than your physical health. You will need to work on the wellbeing of your emotional health through your emotional intelligence. And the best way to start is through self-awareness. As mentioned in the previous chapter, self-awareness is the key to emotional intelligence.

Emotions – the Root!

Emotions are feelings that you need to understand and comprehend. Ask yourself – how do I feel when a particular emotion engulfs me? This is where self-awareness plays its part – you need to be aware of your emotions to decide the next course of action. Similarly, you also need to know how others feel and be aware of their emotions.

There are many ways to tell what feelings (and emotions) another person is experiencing, but the best way is by observing their verbal and non-verbal signals. Studies and research suggest that more than 80 percent of communication is done through facial and body expression, i.e., body language and gestures. Framing your emotions into words is difficult, and most of us often don't like to talk about our emotions. This is why it comes out of your system through body language – most emotions are expressed through body language.

The Brain's Role in Emotions

It isn't possible to consciously control your emotions. The limbic system is the part of the brain that deals with emotions. Scientists and experts believe that this part of the brain evolved pretty early, probably ever since human civilization began on this planet. It is considered primitive, which is why an emotional response is considered clear-cut, but powerful and strong. When you are overwhelmed by emotions, you don't want to talk about it – all you feel like doing is shouting, running away, or crying.

Why does this happen? Emotions are powerful enough to shake your entire system. These emotional responses (crying or shouting or shutting yourself out from the world) are based on the need to survive. Emotions are associated with experience and memory – most of the time, emotions bubble out of your system when you are reminded of your past through an action that happens in the present.

For instance, if you experienced something awful during your childhood, your emotional response to similar incidents (stimulus) is more likely to be stronger. From the time a human is born, emotions become a part of his or her life. Babies feel emotions but are unable to reason why they feel a certain way. Most emotions, whether subtle or strong, are closely linked to your ethics and values. When an emotional response comes out of your system due to a particular action, it means that one of your key values has been challenged. When you understand and comprehend this particular link to values and memory, you can find the key to manage your emotional response. Emotional responses aren't necessarily associated with a current situation – they are mostly your reaction to a past incident or trauma. It is possible to overcome such emotions through reasoning or by being aware of your reactions to such an emotion.

How do you work on this?

- Take some time out from your daily routine to observe your emotional responses.

- Think about what may have caused such responses – is it a memory or a previous experience? Or were your values challenged?

- Differentiate between your positive and negative emotions. Observe what results in negative emotions and what is more positive.

- Remind yourself that it is possible to change how you feel.

When you have high positive energy, you can perform well, but you cannot stay in that jubilant state forever. There is a need to reduce your energy to bring back balance in the system – sooner or later. When you stay positive, you recover overwhelming positive or negative emotions quickly. Dipping too much into negative feelings will make you feel burnt out.

But when you look at high negative energy, it is an uncomfortable and painful place to be. You feel like you're always fighting to survive. There is no enjoyment in life – you fight each day to survive! Just like too much high positive energy is not good, too much negative energy is a definite no-no. You will have to reduce energy at some point in time, or else you will feel the burnout in you.

There are so many ways that can help you manage your emotions, and thankfully most of them are quite generic. You can always try them out because you might find that some of them do work for you.

Exercise regularly

You feel better when you exercise as it releases the pleasure and reward chemicals in your brain, such as dopamine. When you are fit, you are physically healthy. This will help you manage your emotions in a better manner.

Kindness is not an act, and it is a lifestyle

Be kind to everyone. Turn it into a lifestyle. When you are kind to others, you will eventually be kind to yourself too. This will help reduce emotional turmoil – especially the rush of emotions you go through when you worry about yourself.

Acknowledge and accept

Don't slip into criticizing mode immediately! Accept things and learn to appreciate what is going on around you. Be mindful. Practice mindfulness – be aware of what is going on in the present.

Open up and talk

It is good to talk – spend time with your friends or loved ones. Enjoy their company and open up. Don't always shut yourself out!

Get distracted

Don't lock yourself in your room and keep dwelling on the past. Kick the doors open – do something that will help you forget that you were feeling down. Watch TV, go outdoors, browse for some time, watch a movie, read books, play with your pets, do gardening, etc.

Challenge your negative thoughts

Don't give in to negative thinking so easily. If you find yourself thinking too much, challenge your negative thoughts by finding evidence against them.

Get outdoors

Nature is the best therapy to calm down your emotions. Get some fresh air, watch the birds, walk up a hill and look at the view from there. It calms your mind and frees you from negative emotions.

Be grateful

Be grateful for whatever has happened in your life. Remember the good things that have happened. Thank the people who were involved in them. Pay gratitude to your well-wishers for all the nice things they've done for you.

Do things you enjoy

Always play to your strengths and do things that are good for you –
your mind and body. If you like something, do it! For instance, if
you have always wanted to watch the sunrise, wake up early and go
out. Watch the morning sun as he wishes you a good day. Your mind
will clear and your emotions will be much calmer.

Count your blessings

Don't keep fretting or cribbing. Notice all the good things in your
life. Be grateful for it. When you find the right balance, you can work
towards reducing your stress levels, which will ultimately help you
fight depression.

Apply Reason

As mentioned earlier, it is possible to change how you feel. When
you are aware of your emotional response, you get to comprehend
what may be behind it. The moment you can find the source of the
response, you can start applying reason to said situation.

Question yourself about certain responses and possible courses of
action:

- What is it I am feeling about this situation?

- What should I be doing about it?

- Will that decision have any effect on me?

- Will it affect the other people?

- Whatever action I am taking, does it fit with my values and
  ethics?

- If not, how do I make it fit better?

- Should I be asking for help?

The answer to these questions will act as a solution for you in applying a reason behind the said emotional response. This way you don't react but respond!

Imagine you are scared of being in the dark because you were once shut in a dark trapdoor at your grandparent's place when you were a kid. Even today, you fear staying in the dark, which manifests as physical symptoms too – you sweat the moment the light goes off, your hands shiver, and your breathing becomes intense.

You know that this emotional response to darkness is because of your childhood experience. How do you overcome it? Tell yourself that you are no more a feeble child but have grown up. There is nothing that can scare you now. All you've got to do is walk across the dark room, find the power and switch on the lights. When you practice this regularly, you are teaching your brain to understand that there is no need to fear the darkness. When you do this, you re-train your limbic system to overcome your fear.

Decide with emotions

Your decisions can be based on emotions, reasons or a combination of the two. Deciding based on emotions is often believed to be done in the heat of the moment, but when you look at it, most decisions we make are based on emotions. It can be knowingly or unknowingly. For instance, if you are asked to make an important life decision, such as marriage – you will be putting in a great amount of thought before you decide to go ahead with the marriage. However, there are a few who argue that decisions are solely made based on logic.

But the fact is – the best decisions are made both with emotion and logic because if you use either of them, your decisions may not support your emotional needs or may not be balanced. But when you combine your emotional response with rational thought, you can conclude with a satisfying decision.

How do you do this?

- Don't make decisions in haste. Pause and give yourself a chance to think.

- Will the result of each possible action give you satisfaction? Think about the feeling you will undergo.

- Will the decision you make affect others? Will you be happy with those effects? Ponder your thoughts over it.

- Give yourself some time before you finalize your decision.

- If your decision goes against your values or ethics, think about why you made such a choice? Did something feel right about it?

- Think about the reactions of your loved ones when your decision is implemented. Will you be happy with their responses?

- Think about what would happen if everyone around you took similar action, would it lead to a disaster? If yes, drop that decision.

Emotions are a significant part of your life. It is a great blessing to be able to be aware of your feelings, as well as other's feelings. People with high emotional intelligence can do this all the time, and it is a skill that can be practiced and developed.

Self-Management and Emotions

Managing your emotions based on what you know about them is referred to as self-management. You work toward generating positive interactions with people and motivate yourself to navigate through all possible scenarios. The moment you can acknowledge a negative emotion, you are consciously attempting to prevent yourself from losing control over your behavior.

Self-management on emotional quotient is crucial for leadership roles as no one would like to work for a manager who cannot keep his emotional responses under control. If the reaction of a leader always depends on their prevailing mood, it would be difficult to achieve the required result. Achieving the desired results by shouting at your team and bullying your team members will no longer. People know their rights and employment courts do not stand by organizations that allow bullying behavior.

It doesn't mean that you should never be angry. Anger is an emotion, and when you bottle it up, it can become worse. Certain circumstances will demand such an emotional response, and it is perfectly reasonable to use it to get things done. But the key point is – you will need to have control over your anger in such a way that you channel the energy in the right manner to resolve the problem at hand.

Few people have this tendency of exaggerating the emotions in their minds – especially the negative aspects of a particular scenario. For instance, being worried or scared about a meeting you are about to have with an important customer. In case you recognize such a trait in you, you will need to use self-reflection and apply the reflective cycle to such scenarios to make sure you see the reality of it – look at it more logically and realistically.

When you work toward improving your self-control ability, you think about scenarios logically and decide on the potential ways to handle them. This helps you in a long run as you work on reducing your anger or fear that ultimately helps manage your emotions much better!

Three steps that will help improve your self-control are:

Recognizing Your Feeling

It can be a subtle feeling over a missed train or a strong feeling over a missed deliverable. Identify the feeling. This will tell you that you got that feeling in the first place because there was something wrong with the usual environment. Exercising self-awareness in your feelings is the starting point.

Discover the Underlying Cause

This is considered the most difficult step. Why? This process requires proper analysis, self-reflection and honesty to recognize and identify the cause of the feeling. For instance, your boss isn't happy with you because your team missed the deadline for a critical project. What is your feeling? You are angry! Why are you angry? Is it because your boss told you that your team didn't meet the client's expectation? Or is it because your team failed you? Or is it because you think you weren't capable of handling the situation well? Now comes the next question – Who are you angry with? Your boss, your team, or yourself? When you get a clear and honest answer to all these questions, you will finally find the underlying cause of your emotional response.

Time for Action

Now that you have found the underlying cause of your emotion, it is time to take action to set things right. You need to break the cycle of negation emotions that is overpowering you. You need to tell your brain that the emotions you are currently feeling are inappropriate or directed at the wrong target.

Emotional self-control refers to how effectively you can control or manage your behavior on the emotional triggers. If you have strong emotional self-control, you will manage to stay cool-headed and composed, even in stressful situations. This is one critical competency that a leader needs to develop to be efficient as the team reflects the leader's conduct. If you as a leader lose your temper so often, you are creating an atmosphere of fear and irritation in your team that ultimately affects the productivity of the team.

On the contrary, if the leader remains poised under stress, the calm reaction can give confidence to his team, and they would believe that their leader is with them. They feel positive that their leader would help them to get through the situation. In today's business world, calmness and creativity are the only two factors that can solve even the most complex situations.

Tips to Work on Your Emotional Quotient

- Make an honest assessment of your behavior, identify the problem areas and address them before they get destructive. Follow the same with your team too. The behaviors can be either of the following or all of them:

  - Getting influenced by others easily

  - Too much foreshadowing

  - Digging too much on past events

  - Being overcritical

- Looking for the chance to blame others

- Over-thinking or not thinking at all

- Focusing too much on negative feedback

- Overburdening yourself with responsibilities (that are more than what you can handle)

- Acknowledging and accepting your negative behavior is the key to developing your emotional self-management skills. When you have identified a negative behavior in you, you should take positive steps to eliminate the negativity or control the behavior to an extent.

- Most of the time, we as humans are influenced by the attitudes and moods of the people around us. Have you or any of your team members been influenced this way? If yes, you might have to make a conscious effort to cut off yourself from such vibes and get back to your objective.

- Not everyone will have this effect on you, and it is important for you to identify who they are. In most cases, it is the boss or a colleague with whom you have a personal relationship that is in some way more than a professional relationship. It can be a person whom you admire or respect or maybe someone in whom you see too much of yourself.

- If their attitude and mood are positively affecting you, it is good, but if it is too much negativity, then you will have to neutralize this emotion.

- Stop playing out negative scenarios in your head. This usually leads to fear, which in turn generates irrational thoughts, ultimately crippling your decision-making skills.

- It is difficult to break such patterns, as it has been a lifelong habit. But you can do it by imagining a positive outcome to every scenario and thereby refusing to accept habitual doom-and-gloom negative outcomes in your head.

When you concentrate on your behaviors such as conscientiousness and adaptability, you can work towards altering your behavior and in the process, alter your emotional responses too. Be conscious of your emotions and its consequent behavior so that you can use it to your advantage to develop the emotional quotient in you.

Chapter Ten: Unleash The Empath In You!

When you want someone to see things from the other person's perspective, the first thing you will tell him or her is – put yourself in his shoes before you stand on him! This ability to look at something from the other person's perspective and trying to understand what they go through is referred to as empathy.

Empathy is the ability to interact with and lead by comprehending other people's views, feelings and thoughts. When you work on improving your empathy, you become a better human being. Empathy is strongly connected to the emotional quotient in a person. It can lead to a series of advantages such as:

- Succeeding in a professional environment (workplace)

- Stronger and more meaningful personal relationships

- Better quality of life and good health

Around 90 percent of top-performing individuals in most workplaces are said to come with a high emotional quotient. When people are self-aware of their thoughts, emotions and feeling, they are better in understanding the others' too. Listening plays an important role in this. When you listen better with an open mind, you tend to become a better person!

Lack of Empathy and its Negative Effects

Lack of empathy has been linked to criminal behaviors such as murder, robbery, drug dealing, etc. Multiple studies have proved this and claimed that most people in prison lack empathy. These prisoners who have been charged guilty never really cared about their victims. They didn't make any attempt to understand the emotions and feelings their victims were going through. If they had empathy, they wouldn't be in prison in the first place. When a person can empathize with another person, it is quite impossible for him to do anything rash or brutal.

Honesty and Trust

When you empathize with others, you are unconsciously placing your trust in the person. It gives you the ability to trust. When the person feels that you care for him or her, you are successful in earning his or her trust. Trust is important to build a healthy relationship. If your friends trust you, they will be more than willing to take risks for you and the most important of all – they will be honest and open with you! Your friends will talk openly only when they know they can trust you.

When trust builds, exchange of information increases and they will start sharing their thoughts and feelings with you. The trust they have in you might even make them open up the darkest secrets of their life. Gaining such a trust is a blessing nowadays as you hardly see such people around. This doesn't refer solely to friendship – it extends to personal relationships and professional relationships too. If your colleague can trust you such that she doesn't mind sharing her disturbing thoughts with you, you are working pretty well on your emotional quotient. Empathy and trust go hand in hand. Openness and honesty come only when the trust factor is strong.

Being Considerate and Understanding

You are busy playing a game on your mobile when a colleague of yours comes over with a worried look on her face. You stop for a second, look at her and ask her what is wrong. She tells you about a client call that went bad and is worried about the issue escalating. Instead of actively listening to her, you go back to your mobile game and respond to her with hmm's, aha's and oh's. How do you think she would feel? Will she come back to you ever again when she needs a compassionate ear? No, absolutely not! You just showed her that you are not interested in listening to what she has to say. You lost her trust, and you were pathetically inconsiderate and thoughtless.

The basic and simple thing you have to do when someone approaches you to talk about their worries, ideas or interests is to stop whatever you are doing and listen to them. When you are empathetic, you are aware of the feeling that is being shown. When you are approached for help, try to comprehend and understand what is not being said (nonverbal cues) along with what is being said (the verbal conversation).

Most important emotions in a conversation are conveyed through nonverbal signals such as body language, gestures, facial expression, tone of the voice, etc. You may not realize that every single movement in the body sends a message. The most important part of empathy is to understand nonverbal messages and show consideration for the feeling they are going through. You become an effective communicator when you can empathize and understand what the other person needs from you. Learn to comprehend nonverbal messages to discover more about the other person's thoughts and emotions.

The most common examples of nonverbal communication are:

- Facial expressions

- Eye contact

- Physical touch or contact

- Bodily appearance (physical)

- Hand gestures or physical actions

- The different sounds a person usually makes (depending on the emotions).

Empathy lays the rock-solid foundation for better emotional intelligence, and it is possible to improve your empathy through regular practice. You need to follow the right process and religiously practice them to take your empathy to the next level, which will help increase your overall emotional intelligence. You don't have to go through an expensive course or a complicated process to learn empathy. Choose the right resources and tools!

Why Practice Empathy?

Practicing empathy will help you with greater success professionally and personally, as it is one of the fundamental factors that are required to improve your emotional intelligence. The more empathetic you are, the happier you become! Why is it necessary to specifically work toward enhancing your ability to empathize with others?

- You will begin to treat people the way you want to be treated and more importantly, you would treat the people you care about exactly the way they wish to be treated.

- You will be smart enough to understand the wants and needs of the people around you.

- You can understand the perception others have about you based your actions and words.

- You can comprehend the unspoken words of people and respond similarly.

- You can successfully adhere to your customer's needs, as

you are aware of what they are looking for.

- Interpersonal conflicts – both at work and at home - will be fewer as you can deal with them in a better manner.

- Your accurate prediction of people's actions and reactions will be helpful to work on your next course of action/

- You will be self-motivated and make extra efforts to motivate the people around you.

- Your convincing skills will improve, as you can influence your ideas and suggestions effectively.

- You will always allow two-way communication as you start looking at the perspectives and perceptions of the people around you.

- Handling negative people will no longer be an issue as you are better at comprehending their fears and motivations. You begin to empathize by putting yourself in their shoes and work towards a constructive solution.

- You not only become a better leader or a better friend but on the whole, you become a better person!

How to Practice Empathy?

There are a few simple ideas you can follow to develop your empathy, and they are,

- Stop and listen

- Observe and marvel

- Recognize your enemies

- Be the third person

Stop and Listen

Listen with rapt attention when people talk to you. Active listening is important; stop whatever you are doing and get into listening mode. Most often, conversations are often only talking with no listening – this happens when there is a heated discussion or arguments on sensitive topics. Often, people keep talking back and forth with each other, listening enough to reply to the other person's argument or statement. Sometimes, they don't even pause to listen; it is just back and forth talking at each other.

You will also be able to recognize such a pattern within yourself when you think deeper. You will have the response formulated in your head waiting to spit it out the moment the other person has finished with his or her sentence. It will look like you are in for a war of words where each party wants to make sure his or her word is the final.

When you find yourself being part of such a conversation, don't rush - slow down. Push yourself hard to listen to the words the other person is speaking. Gauge the motto (reason or objective) of the speaker behind what he or she is saying and why he or she is saying so. Think what led to this thought process in him – maybe his work experience and the way he was brought up has led to his current viewpoint.

Don't be a mute spectator; respond visually with body languages and gestures such as making eye contact, nodding your head, etc. You can also respond with sounds such as oh, aha, hmm, ok, etc. but let the second pass before you respond verbally. Before you respond with your reply, ask follow-up questions to make sure what the speaker intended and what you understood are the same, which will also help you understand their current emotional state.

Since you were completely focused on the speaker, you will need some to time to speak or respond, as you are yet to prepare your response for the same.

Observe and Marvel

Don't always stick your head into your mobile or iPad. Instead of checking your Facebook or WhatsApp while waiting for your train or when you are stuck in traffic, look around! Observe the people around you and imagine who they might be, what they might be feeling, what might be running in their head, where are they headed to now, etc. Is the person on that yellow bike happy? Is he frustrated? Is he humming the song he is listening to through his earphones? Does he have similar problems as me? Is that lady worried about some meeting she is expecting this noon? Is that why there is a worried look on her face? Just gaze around. Try to observe and marvel!

Recognize Your Enemies

Enemies might be an exaggerated word here, but think about an ongoing dispute you are having with someone – maybe your team member who is trying to disrupt your work routine to prove she is better. Or maybe a particular family member who is constantly coming up with conflictive arguments for whatever you do or say. You always have this thought in your head that whatever they do or say is wrong and you are right – whoever it is (maybe a colleague or family member). Because you are on the opposite side of the war field, you tend to disagree with them on anything and everything, irrespective of what they are arguing for!

Now, reverse the roles – imagine the entire scenario from the other person's perspective. The person isn't evil or a complete fool. Maybe they aren't wrong about whatever you disagree about. The problem here is more to do with the basic philosophical (ideological) difference between you than about the particular conflict that is taking place between both of you.

How does the other person feel when you disagree with them? Are they affected emotionally by the way you respond? What is causing the fear in the other person to accept or reason out with you? How do you worsen those fears in them instead of calming them? Are there any valid agreements for the person to make against your viewpoint? If so, what are they? Does this person hold any good intentions for you? Do they have any positive motivations behind what you think to be negative? If so, what are they? Do you agree with them? Do think these motivations hold more importance than the particular conflict between you two?

When you do this exercise a couple of times, you will feel your irritation and anger reducing – especially with the interpersonal situations which is stressing both of you. It may look clear, but it is different when you do it.

Be the Third Person

It can be difficult and tough to side with your enemy, so it is best to choose the other side – the third side. Look at the entire scenario from a third person's perspective. This step will require a lot of discipline, as you will already be stressed about your own emotions and thoughts. To make things easy, try it with an actual third person.

All of us have loved ones and friends who come to us to complain about that person who has been treating them badly. It is common for humans to complain, as it is the basic nature of the species. It is also the duty of the friend or loved one to listen to the complaints and be sympathetic or compassionate toward the complainer. The general assumption is that the listener will side with the complainer and support him or her. And psychologically speaking, a person who is caring and supportive will side with the complainer, but will also point out the arguments of the other person!

Try practicing this – complain about your opponent to the third person. But don't go with your default reaction immediately. Vent your emotions and then start reflecting. Once you finish with your side of the argument, you become the opposite person and start complaining about yourself. State points from the other person's perspective. Work your way back. This way, you force yourself to hear and speak for your opponent.

All this finally comes down to one major factor – empathy. Though we read a lot of articles and hear a lot of speeches about this, I wonder if people practice empathy – including myself. But if you want to bring a positive change to your emotional health, practicing empathy for even a short period should do the magic.

Tips to Improve Empathy

Research and studies show that empathy is partly inherent and partly learned. It is indeed possible to improve your empathy. There are eight ways to strengthen it, and they are:

Get out of your comfort zone and challenge yourself

When you stick to your comfort zone, you find fewer opportunities to learn and grow. Take up more challenges and experience the change you are undergoing, especially when you are no more in your protective and comfortable zone. Learn a new skill maybe – playing the piano or learning a new language or developing a new competency. When you do such things, you will become humble as you are pushed to stay grounded to learn new things – things that you have no clue about! Modesty enables empathy!

Travel and change of place impart new vigor to the mind (Seneca)

Move away from your usual environment. Travel to new places and explore their culture, since it will make you appreciate even the little things in others.

Ask for Feedback

I know I've been repeating this for quite a while now, but it is important – getting feedback is the only way for you to change and grow. Get feedback on your relationship skills from colleagues, family and friends. Listen to what they have to say and work on improving your lagging areas. Check with them to see how you are doing on a periodic basis.

Explore not just the head, but the heart too

Read books that talk about emotions, read literature that explores romantic relationships or personal connections. This is said to improve empathy – a study conducted on young doctors proved that reading literature showed improved empathy in them.

Put yourself in other's shoes

Initiate a conversation with people and find out what it's like to walk in their shoes. Talk about their concerns and ideas. Check how they handled the situations. Sometimes you will feel like your problems are much better compared to the others.

Inspect your partiality

Everyone has hidden biases within them and sometimes it is not so hidden. When you are biased or partial toward a party, you will lose the ability to decide rationally. It interferes with your ability to empathize, and most often these biases are centered on evident factors such as race, age, gender. Are you partial to a particular group? No? Think again – all of us are!

Be curious

What can I learn from a fresher? What can I learn from a client who is always self-centered? Cultivate the habit of asking curious questions. The right questions can lead you toward a stronger understanding of people.

Ask thoughtful questions

Don't ask questions just for the sake of it. Even if your questions are provocative, let them be thoughtful.

How to be Empathetic

A recent discovery by the neuroscientists has proved that the multiple systems of mirror neurons in human brains are responsible for experiencing empathy. These mirror neurons reflect the actions we examine in others, causing us to imitate the same action in our brains. For instance, when you see someone in pain, you experience the same emotion to an extent. Similarly, when you are with a person who is in an extremely joyful mood, you reflect the same emotion within you to a particular extent. The fundamental physiological bases of empathy are the mirror neurons. They produce a neural Wi-Fi that helps you to connect with people's feelings around you.

Though the majority of the people are naturally empathetic, there are the others who are not. But fortunately, empathy can be learned – research shows that this particular trait, even if not inborn, can be cultivated through regular practice. But to achieve this trait and to practice, you will need to overcome few potential blockades. They are:

Barricade 1 – Not focusing

Your mirror neurons kick in strongest when you notice and examine a person's emotions – eye gestures, body position, facial expressions and physical appearance. Most often people are distracted by their thoughts or other stuff that they fail to pay attention to a person – especially when you multitask.

Solution

Remind yourself of the importance of empathy and how it can lead to success in your personal and professional life. Motivate yourself to empathize with the scenario and people. Put away electronic gadgets and get into active listening mode. Fine-tune your observation skills, especially the nonverbal cues such as a quick change in facial expressions, uncomfortable body postures, trying to read the eyes of the person, etc.

Try to improve your nonverbal understanding by watching subtle dramas or movies with low volume. Make an effort to understand what each character is saying and read what the character is emoting.

Barricade 2 – Communication Issue

Not knowing how to communicate empathetically even after feeling his or her emotions.

Solution

Work on your nonverbal expressions; make a conscious effort to notice what you do (nonverbally) while interacting with people. Check your micro-expressions, hand movement, body postures, etc. Ask your friends to give you honest feedback on your nonverbal communication, especially in situations when you are overwhelmed by emotions.

Check if you have difficulty in being empathetic with specific people. If so, observe and understand why it happens. Concentrate on your tones. When people like teachers, friends, politicians, etc. are empathizing with others, listen to their tone.

I am sorry that you had to go through this. – Try saying this sentence in various ways with different voice tones. See if you feel empathetic when you hear yourself say it.

Be smart enough to leave people alone when they want to be left alone. Don't force your presence and empathetic words upon them. They might not want it at that particular time. For instance, if your friend who is going through a terrible phase because of her divorce proceedings is sending you signals to say that she doesn't want to talk now, respect her feelings and leave her alone.

Barricade 3 – Not able to show empathy

There are times when you do not feel the same way another person is feeling, but your brain is instructing you to be empathetic and hear the person out. This is referred to as cognitive empathy.

Solution

You can always disagree with someone and yet understand the

feeling they are going through. Sometimes it is more important to listen to someone and not judge them since this will help them realize that you are empathetic towards them. Communicate honestly in a way that makes the other person feel that you genuinely understand what he or she feels.

Articulating Your Emotions or Feelings

Extroverts usually have the natural gift of being better at letting go of their emotions and feelings, because they are good with words. But concentration, practice and perseverance can help the others who come without this natural gift. When you can express the emotions then and there through body language or writing or by talking with other people, you are giving no chances for your health to dysfunction.

Researchers have found that it is beneficial to release and let go of emotions. Multiple studies have proved that repressed negative emotions or bottled up emotions can lead to increased stress. These researches also suggest that writing about feelings will give better health outcomes for people who have experienced traumatic events, asthma patients and breast-cancer patients. There was also a study conducted on people who lived for 100 years. The result of the study was their positive attitude towards life, and healthy emotional expression has led them to live for many years.

Therefore, it is better to articulate and express your feelings and emotions to maintain physical and emotional health. If you are someone who often finds it difficult to let go of these emotions, it is time you work on the emotional quotient in you. That being said, the solution is not to pop the top off that bottle of emotions and allowing it to spray all over the place. If you do that, you can never identify the cause of a problem or situation!

Conclusion

We have come to the end of the book. Thank you once again for choosing this book.

I sincerely hope this book was useful and helped you as a reader to get a clear and good understanding of emotional intelligence. This book provides information on what emotional intelligence is and why it is important to you. It also helps you understand the impact emotional intelligence has on you and your surrounding environment. The chapters will provide you with important guidelines on how to apply emotional intelligence in handling professional relationships at the workplace and how to avoid strained personal relationships. The book dwells on the importance of self-awareness, self-control, self-reflection and self-motivation to enhance one's emotional intelligence.

I hope this book has helped to answer the many questions you may have had about emotional intelligence.

Thank you and best wishes!

P.S

Never stop working on your emotional intelligence and abilities. Always take time out to practice self-awareness and most importantly, keep that learning spirit burning always!

1 305 925 3034

(250-69-003) 250 - 66. 945

101 001 614 022

2,050 points

15-18
Grand Vista
Orlando

Made in the USA
San Bernardino, CA
14 September 2018